361.7 HEN
3524500032 041   1998
14s
Henley, Michael J.
Fund raising & marketing in
the one-person shop :
achieving success with
limited resources / by

PUBLIC LIBRARY
GREENFIELD WI

Fund Raising
& Marketing in the
One-Person Shop

Achieving Success
With Limited Resources

Michael J. Henley & Diane L. Hodiak

Development Resource Center
Minneapolis, Minnesota

D1410452

The authors have worked to the best of their ability to ensure the accuracy of the materials represented in this book. We assume no responsibility for errors, inaccuracies, or omissions. Any perceived slight to any individual or organization is unintentional. Readers should use their own judgement applying this material to their own situation and contacting an expert if appropriate.

©1997, Michael J. Henley and Diane L. Hodiak

ALL RIGHTS RESERVED. No part of this publication may be reproduced, stored in a retrieval system, or transmitted by any means, mechanical, photocopy, electronic, recording, or otherwise without the prior written permission of the authors and publisher.

Library of Congress Catalog number 97-91585.

ISBN 09657161-0-4.

First edition, printed July 1997.

Publisher's Cataloging-in-Publication
(Provided by Quality Books, Inc.)

Henley, Michael J.
    Fund Raising and marketing in the one-person shop; achieving success with limited resources Michael Henley, Diane Hodiak-1st ed.
    p.cm.
    Includes index.
    Preassigned LCCN; 97-91585
    ISBN; 0-9657161-0-4

    1. Fund raising 2.Volunteers-Recruiting 3. Nonprofit organizations--Finance 4. Nonprofit organizations--Marketing I. Hodiak, Diane II. Title

HV41.2H46 1997   361.7'068'1
                      QB197-40536

Attention all school groups, institutions, colleges, universities and professional associations:
Quantity discounts are available for bulk purchases for purposes of education, fund raising, or gift giving to staff, board, and volunteers. Special books, inserts, or excerpts can be prepared to meet your needs. For more information, contact the authors at Development Resource Center, 4744-10th Avenue South, Minneapolis, MN 55407. Phone: 612-825-0735, fax: 612-929-1736.

Fund Raising & Marketing in the One-Person Shop

GREENFIELD PUBLIC LIBRARY
7215 WEST COLDSPRING RD
GREENFIELD, WI 53220

*To Victor and Agnes Henley, whose lifelong example of sharing time,
talent, and financial resources has inspired family, friends, and community.*

To Kaitlin and Benjamin who are following that example.

*To Joanna and Danielle, that you might learn
the responsibilities and joy of giving.*

ACKNOWLEDGMENTS

The ability to bring a book to publication requires much more than dedication of the authors. Equally necessary is the support of colleagues, friends, and family.

We thank the small group of initial reviewers, development managers who spent considerable time reading the initial draft, for indicating their preferences for clarification and content. We are grateful to Lisa Anderson, Mary Hartnett, Barbara Krinke, Russell Langsam, Kari Luther Carlson, Chris Mayer, Marcia McDonald, Mary Quirk, Patrick Shields, Robert Voigt, and Randi S. N. Yoder. You have helped us to create a book that we feel meets the needs of others like you, who are currently working in the field.

As well, we appreciate those nonprofit managers who were surveyed early in the book's development, providing us with necessary details about their needs. In this list we include: Lisa Anderson, Mary Ann Boe, Julie R. Brown, Kari Luther Carlson, Mark Haidet, Mary Hassing, Sister Virginia Hinks, Kevin R. Johnson, Thomas Keefe, Dennis F. Kelly, Audrey P. Kintzi, Anne L. Long, Thaddeus Ludwiczak, Linda S. Moore, Carolyn Nelson, Karen Scheibner, Patrick Shields, Carol Stoddart, Dawn Halverson Sursely, Cynthia Theis, Sarah Milligan-Toffler, Joann Usher, Laura Waterman Wittstock, J. Zark, and Cathy Zimmerman.

Equally important are the development managers whose case studies appear herein. We are grateful that they have shared their expertise and success so that other managers might also prosper.

We wish to specifically thank Henry Rosso, who has been a mentor and inspiration to many who work in the field of fund raising. We deeply appreciate his unselfish devotion to bringing excellence to nonprofit managers and volunteers. His support, early in the development of this book, provided us with the courage to proceed, and the inspiration to finish.

Lastly, our families have shared the burden of bringing this book to press. We appreciate their encouragement and willingness to help us succeed.

ABOUT THE AUTHORS

Michael J. Henley, CFRE

Michael Henley has served the nonprofit sector for more than thirty years. His extensive career experience, throughout the United States and abroad, has included management and development experience with nonprofit organizations such as Little Brothers - Friends of the Elderly, Ronald McDonald House, Junior Achievement, American Refugee Committee, and the Peace Corps. He has worked as a direct service provider, program manager, executive director, and as president of a local and national board of directors. Most importantly, Mr. Henley has professionally managed the growth and development of several one and two-person development shops.

Skilled in a number of fund raising capacities, Mr. Henley is knowledgeable about the how-to's of managing capital campaigns, planned giving programs, endowments and special event programs for the small to medium-size development shop.

Diane L. Hodiak, M.B.A.

With more than twenty years experience in marketing and public relations, Diane Hodiak is an expert resource. She has been a trainer for the Wilder Foundation and the University of St.Thomas in St. Paul, Minnesota, director of public relations and development for CampFire Boys and Girls, as well as the executive director of three human service organizations.

Presently, Diane Hodiak provides counsel to nonprofit organizations in the areas of marketing, planning, public relations, and fund development. Her clients include churches, school districts, membership organizations, community groups, and other nonprofit organizations. Particularly successful in developing cost-effective individual donor acquisition and cultivation campaigns, Ms. Hodiak often counsels nonprofit organizations in the conceptual development and implementation of direct mail campaigns, including list brokerage services. An award-winning writer, she also provides copywriting services. Additionally, Diane Hodiak's ability to strategically plan and develop winning grant proposals has helped many nonprofit organizations to win major grants.

Michael Henley and Diane Hodiak provide consulting services to nonprofit organizations, churches, foundations, school districts, associations, and membership societies. If you are interested in obtaining more information about services in fund raising, direct marketing, list purchasing, strategic marketing, or public relations, you may reach them at:

Development Resource Center
4744 10th Avenue South
Minneapolis, MN 55410
612-825-0735   612-929-6737

LIST OF ILLUSTRATIONS

Illustration 1:	Key Players; Development Program	3
Illustration 2:	Volunteer Bill of Rights	5
Illustration 3:	Volunteer Responsibilities	9
Illustration 4:	Prospect Rating Form	21
Illustration 5-1:	ARC Home Page	37
Illustration 5-2:	ARC Home Page	38
Illustration 6:	SWOT Analysis	51
Illustration 7:	Key Competitor Analysis	54
Illustration 8:	Service Configuration Matrix	55
Illustration 9:	Constituency Circle	56
Illustration 10-1:	Child's Play Theatre Company(Member Survey); Page 1..65	
Illustration 10-2:	Child's Play Theatre Company(Member Survey); Page 2..66	
Illustration 11-1:	Child's Play Theatre Company(Group Survey); Page 1... 67	
Illustration 11-2:	Child's Play Theatre Company(Group Survey); Page 2... 68	
Illustration 12:	Key Public Matrix	71
Illustration 13-1:	Emergency FoodShelf Network; Letter, Page 1	77
Illustration 13-2:	Emergency FoodShelf Network; Letter, Page 2	78
Illustration 13-3:	Emergency FoodShelf Network; Brochure	79
Illustration 13-4:	Emergency FoodShelf Network; Reply Device	80
Illustration 13-5:	Emergency FoodShelf Network; Envelope	81
Illustration 14:	Board Member Job Description	86
Illustration 15:	Protocol Sheet	93
Illustration 16:	Sample Press Release	97
Illustration 17:	Sample Media Advisory Letter	98
Illustration 18:	Giving Pyramid	121
Illustration 19-1:	Children's Home Society; Radio Program Pledge Card	136
Illustration 19-2:	Children's Home Society; Radio Program Solicitation Card	137
Illustration 19-3:	Children's Home Society; Letter	138
Illustration 19-4:	Children's Home Society; Direct Mail Reply Device	139
Illustration 19-5:	Children's Home Society; Exterior and Return Envelope	140
Illustration 20:	Telemarketing Pledge Chart	165
Illustration 21:	Gift Club Acknowledgment	179

We dedicate this book to you, development managers, executive directors, church officers and volunteers, staff of membership societies, foundations and associations, and public agencies and institutions. Most of you operate alone or with minimal staffing support. Although many of your goals may be vastly different, there is one goal that you all share in common: to use your resources wisely in service to the public.

Today more than ever, nonprofit managers face new assaults upon their ability to raise funds and garner support. Competition is greater than ever before. Successfully standing apart from the competition may be the nonprofit manager's most monumental challenge. In order to address this need, we will help you to evaluate and implement detailed planning systems. A solid planning foundation will help you to position your organization in this challenging marketplace and develop successful strategies in marketing and fund raising.

Perhaps you may feel that your many responsibilities often seem to divide your efforts. We hope that our book will provide fresh, new ideas to help you manage your time and resources. In our interviews and work with nonprofit managers, we discovered that those who were happiest with their work had developed powerful systems of coping with lack of staff and financial resources. Many have learned how to integrate methods of fund raising, marketing and public relations in order to interest new donors, cultivate existing constituencies, and raise more money than ever before.

In addition to the case examples from other nonprofit organizations we will also share our own personal insights, gained from a combined experience of more that 40 years in marketing, development, and public relations. We will explain how you can make the most of a limited staff, how you can enlist the support of others, how you can be creative with a limited budget, how you can develop efficient management systems, and how you can use new techniques and technologies to facilitate your many responsibilities. Many of these ideas have come from our own consulting and work experiences with nonprofit groups and organizations of all shapes and sizes.

This book is filled with practical, field-tested solutions. We hope that the creative ideas presented in low-cost marketing communications and designing cost-effective communications will help you extend the impact of your existing budget and increase your overall results. As well, we will present other suggestions to help you enlist the talent and time of others in order to garner increased visibility and support for your organization.

Some of our readers have purchased the book as a training manual for volunteers, board, and staff new to the field. As well, we have also heard positive comments from many experienced managers who benefited from the explanation of emerging trends and technologies and the detailed explanation of marketing planning and implementation. Whatever your situation, we hope that this book will build your enthusiasm, results, and satisfaction. We wish you the best in achieving your goals and the wonderful sense of personal achievement that comes with success.

CONTENTS

CHAPTER 1
HUMAN RESOURCES 1

Admit That You Can't Do It All 1
Setting Priorities 2
Ownership of Marketing and Development 2
The Value of Volunteers 4
Building a Volunteer Base 5
Volunteer Responsibilities 7
Internships 9
How to Recruit Valuable Board Members 9
Collaborations that Enlarge Your Possibilities 10
The "Tom Sawyer" Approach 11
Professional Associations 13

CHAPTER 2
RESEARCH 14

Developing a Donor Profile: Clues and Techniques 14
Telephone Surveys 14
Written Surveys 15
Focus Groups 15
Prospect Research on a Shoestring Budget 16
Detective Work with Envelopes and Checks 17
CD-Rom Databases 17
Organization Annual Reports 17
Form 990's 18
Special Event Programs 18
Corporate and Foundation Annual Reports 18
Newspapers: Business Section 18
Donor Plaques and Donor Walls 19
Prospect Rating 19
Networking 19
Prospect Research Committees 20
Discover the Prospect Researcher Hidden in Your Computer 22
On-Line Services to Support Fund Raising 24

CHAPTER 3
TECHNOLOGY 26

Getting Started: Conduct a Needs Assessment 27
How to Secure Grants for Technology 29
Donated Software 29
Gifts in Kind America 30
Should you Customize or Buy Off the Shelf? 31
Obtaining Computer Hardware at Low or No Cost 31
Should You Go On-line? 32

INTERNET Resources 33
Education/Training/Information 33
Communications Equipment for On-line Services 34
Cost Considerations 34
Services to Meet Your Unique Needs 34
World Wide Web Home Page 36
How to Create a Successful Web Site or Home Page 39
Cost-Saving Multimedia Advances 39
Interactive Television 40
OCR Scanners 40
Digital Cameras 40
Compact Disc Interactive (CDI) Technology 41

CHAPTER 4
PLANNING: THE KEY TO SUCCESS 44

The Importance of Realistic Planning 44
The Strategic Plan 46
What to Expect from a Strategic Planning Process 47
Case Statement 48
The Mission Statement 49
The SWOT Analysis 49
Research: The Key Competitor Analysis 52
Service Configuration Matrix 53
Constituency Circle 53
Evaluation 57

CHAPTER 5
PUBLIC RELATIONS & MARKETING 61

Customer Communications Take Center Stage 62
The Public Relations Plan 69
Explanation for Key Public Matrix 70
Public Relations and the Individual Donor 72
Donor/Member Segmentation Strategies 82
Public Relations and the Board: Nine Easy Ideas 85
Public Relations and the Employee 87
Public Relations and Your External Publics 88
Effective Crisis Management 88
Simple Steps for Effective Media Relations 94
How to Develop a Press Kit 94
The Press Release 94
The Media Advisory Letter 95
When to Mail Your Press Kit 95
Following up With the Right People: The Key to Success 96
Conducting the Interview 100
The Print Media 101

Newspaper Feature Articles 102
Letters to the Editor 103
Designing Cost Effective Marketing Communications 103
Ideas for Low-Cost Marketing Communications 104
Grocery/Discount Stores 104
Display Advertising 105
Statement Stuffers 106
Readerboards 106
Bulletins at Places of Worship 107
Company and Association Newsletters 107
Shopping Center Signs 107
Movie Theaters 107
Rental Video Tapes 108
Piggy-Backing on Others' Promotions 108
Packaging Promotion 108
Stadium Scoreboards 109
Mass Transit 109
Cable Television 109
Video-Tape Productions 110
Placemats or Tent Cards 111
Tips for Trade Shows, State Fairs and Special Events 111
Cross Promotions 113
Key Questions to Help You Plan Successful Events 114

CHAPTER 6
MAJOR GIFTS

MAJOR GIFTS 119

Individual Gifts 119
The Giving Pyramid 119
How to Identify Major Gift Donors for Your Organization 120
Starting a Major Gifts Program 122
How to Cultivate Major Donors 123
Including Other Members of Your Donor's Family 124
How to Identify Major Gift Prospects Outside Your Organization 124
Planned Giving Basics 124
Life Income Gifts 126
Other Planned Gifts 126
Planned Giving for the One-Person Shop 126
Starting Simple With a Wills and Bequests Program 127
Forms of Bequest 128
Specific Outright Bequest 128
Residuary or Remainder Bequest 128
Contingent Bequest 129
Endowment Fund 129
Grants From Foundations 130
Grant Research 130
Persistence Pays Off 132

CHAPTER 7
DONOR SOLICITATION & COMMUNICATIONS..........134

Make It Easy For Your Donors To Give 134
Credit Cards 134
Electronic Fund Transfer 141
Payroll Deduction 141
Evaluating Promotional Results 144
Printed Key Codes 144
Colored marker method 144
Colored dot 145
Bar-coding 145
Is Direct Mail Appropriate for Your Organization? 145
Timing and Frequency 147
Consider Management Costs 147
How to Secure Names for Prospecting 148
Everything You Ever Wanted To Know About Lists 148
Which Lists Are the Best or TESTING 1-2-3 150
Cutting your Mailing Costs By Effective File Management 155
Automation Compatible Mail 156
Deceased File 156
Technology in Marketing Management 157
How to Expand the Number of Lists Through Database Segmentation 158
Appending Information to the Database 160
Profitable Marketing and Fund Raising Ideas 161
Memorial and Tribute Programs 161
Donor/Member Premiums 162
Direct Response 162
Giving Clubs (Major Gifts) 162
Telemarketing 163
Matching Gifts 166
"Marriage Mail" Programs 167
Piggyback Programs 167
Newspaper Inserts 168
More New Ideas From the Field 168

CHAPTER 8
COST SAVINGS 172

Sources for In-Kind Contributions 172
Sources for In-kind Services 173
Barter and Joint Purchasing Agreements 174
The Wish List 175

CHAPTER 9
ACKNOWLEDGMENT & RECOGNITION..........178

Donor and Volunteer Acknowledgment 178

Gift Clubs 178
Timeliness of Acknowledgment 180
Time-saving Acknowledgment Cards 180
Low-cost Variations for Plaques and Certificates 186
Donor Walls 187

HUMAN RESOURCES

■ *Involving Others*

■ *Value of Volunteers*

■ *Internships*

■ *Board Recruitment*

■ *Collaborations*

CHAPTER

1

Introduction

Every organization has limits to its capabilities. This is particularly true of the small development shop. It is vitally important that you realize your limitations. At the same time, you must develop new methods to achieve success with limited resources. Equally important is the necessity of building awareness of the shared responsibility for development with key staff and volunteers.

Taking a few key steps will ensure greater involvement of others and your resultant success.

Admit That You Alone Can't Do It All

The key to success in a small development shop is to realize that you cannot work alone. When all the focus of your organization's development success is on you, you bear a disproportionate share of the burden.

This is why it is so important for you, as a professional, to recognize your personal limitations.

You may want to personally maintain detailed donor records on index cards or a computer; write dozens of funding proposals; develop and mail your annual appeal; maintain relations with the media and the press; acknowledge all donors' gifts; write newsletters and annual reports; meet with donor prospects; organize and conduct several special events; expand your planned giving and endowment programs; and maintain other administrative responsibilities within your organization. Yet, no single individual can do it all.

You, as a professional, must recognize your unique strengths and capabilities and build upon them. Furthermore, you should

Maintaining a "can do" attitude that motivates others, yet is also realistic about the capabilities available, is a supreme challenge.

avoid setting up systems, tasks, or programs that cannot be maintained.

It is also very important for your organization to realize the limits of your development office. This will allow realistic expectations to be set for your job and alleviate the misunderstanding and frustration that can occur when people within your organization think that you can or should do more.

Setting Priorities

Development staff and volunteers need to assist their organizations in setting realistic expectations and establishing priorities for marketing and development efforts. Involve your administrators, development and marketing committees, your board, and key volunteers and donors in this ongoing exercise. Integrate these activities into your current work plans as well as your ongoing strategic plan.

Once you have established these priorities with your key staff and volunteers, it will be much easier for you to politely say no to projects that don't fit within the plan. For example, if your board president attends a special event for another organization and then would like to see your organization do something similar, you may wish to ask, "What should I *not* do in our plan in order to undertake this new activity?" If it does not fit within the plan and you cannot find

a project that you are willing to eliminate, or you can find no other person or group to carry out the activity, then you must learn to say no.

The ability to say no to inappropriate projects helps your organization and your own personal performance evaluation. Isn't it better to be evaluated on development goals that are mutually agreed upon by you, administrators, committees, and the board, at the beginning of the year, than to be measured on impromptu expectations that distract from the overall plan?

Ownership of Marketing and Development

Who is responsible for marketing and development in your organization? The answer should be, everyone!

Everyone in your organization plays a role in increasing public awareness, promoting programs and services, and securing the volunteer, in-kind, and financial resources needed.

The volunteers who greet office visitors or the receptionist who interacts with the public are vitally important to your organization's image and success. Your program staff represent your mission and services to the public every day. Clerical staff who respond to inquiries from the public and send acknowledgments to donors play an important role in the cultivation and involvement of supporters. Your financial directors and staff play an important role in how they interact with your vendors. Your administrators are integral to public relations and the organization's relationships with its donors.

If you continually involve people from all levels of your organization in planning, setting goals, establishing priorities, and carrying out activities, you will increase their sense of ownership and commitment to your marketing and development program. Equally important is a commitment to training for staff and volunteers.

Inform your key staff and volunteers about your department's successes and failures. Sharing this information will, in the long run, help you to secure their ongoing support.

Sometimes development staff find themselves playing the dual role of executive director and development director. In other cases, the development manager may need to help the executive in becoming a more effective supporter of the development effort.

There are many critical roles played by the chief executive. This individual plays a key role in the cultivation, solicitation, and recognition of major donors and donor prospects. The

executive director is also integral to your marketing strategies and may be your key representative in relating to the press and media.

If your executive director is lacking confidence or skills in this area, you need to be encouraging and supportive in helping to develop more effective techniques and skills needed to improve his or her performance. A supportive volunteer, board member,

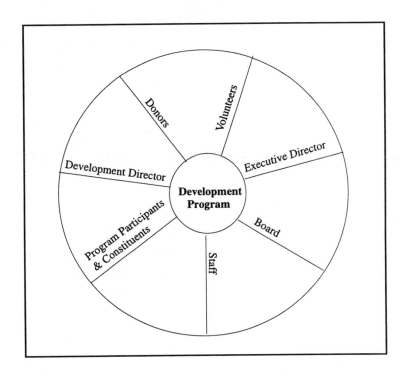

Illustration 1: Key Players; Development Program

or donor may also assist you by encouraging your executive director to attend special training seminars. Or, your executive might be willing to be coached by a peer or mentor.

The Value of Volunteers

In a small development shop with limited resources, volunteers are your most valuable resource. They can make the difference between a successful, mediocre, or weak development program. Volunteers bring new talent, fresh ideas, and renewed energy.

Volunteers may even lead the fund raising effort in smaller organizations, relying upon staff for assistance. In this situation, the members of the board of directors or other key volunteers often assume the responsibility of securing funding for the organization. The staff offers assistance in carrying out the development activities, but actual ownership of the development program lies with the volunteers.

It is necessary to make an initial investment of time and effort to adequately prepare volunteers for their jobs. This investment returns itself ten-fold in the long term.

Volunteers who are provided clear expectations, written job descriptions, and proper orientation and training can assume leadership for major projects. Talented and committed volunteer leaders can recruit and involve others in the work of your organization and carry out activities such as: organizing and conducting special events; designing, producing, and mailing annual appeals, newslet-

ters and annual reports; identifying, cultivating and soliciting major donor prospects; publicly representing the organization as a member of a speakers' bureau; maintaining donor records; mailing acknowledgments; and sponsoring donor recognition events.

In addition to their gifts of time and talent, volunteers are one of the best sources of donors for an organization. What better group of donor prospects do you have than individuals who understand and believe in your mission, advocate your programs and services, and are personally involved and committed to your organization?

Surprisingly, volunteers are often an overlooked or under-used financial resource for many nonprofit groups. Volunteer coordinators and program staff may resist the involvement of the development office with "their" volunteers, and administrators may feel uncomfortable asking people who give so much of their time to also contribute their financial resources.

Nonetheless, it is your responsibility as development staff to help other staff and volunteers understand the importance of volunteer financial support. Therefore, you should regularly offer your volunteers the opportunity to share in the joy of supporting your organization.

Building a Volunteer Base

Where can you find volunteers to assist your small development shop? The first place to look is right around you: your board members, office volunteers, program volunteers, program participants, service recipients, co-workers, family, and friends. Your organization may have a volunteer coordinator and a well-organized volunteer office for program volunteers. Consider asking these volunteers to participate in fund raising and development. If you are enthusiastic, you can easily inspire others to participate and share your enthusiasm.

Illustration 2: Volunteer Bill of Rights

1. To have a prompt, personal interview with your supervisor.

2. To be assigned a job that is worthwhile and challenging and that will use your skills or help you develop new ones.

3. To have a clear understanding of the job, including requirements and responsibilities.

4. To be given a copy of the volunteer job description.

5. To receive orientation to the staff, facilities, and program.

6. To have periodic evaluations of your volunteer service, with upgrading or change of assignment when feasible or desirable.

7. To be informed of the kind of records or documentation the agency will keep for you.

8. To be informed of agency benefits such as reimbursement for out-of-pocket expenses and insurance, and tax deductions allowable for volunteer experience.

9. To receive regular recognition both formally and informally.

10. To be kept informed of what is going on in the agency.

11. To ask for a new assignment, or speak to your supervisor when you want to explore other volunteer opportunities.

Don't forget that volunteers are your best recruiters.

Churches, synagogues, corporations, fraternal organizations, civic associations, and retiree groups can also be an invaluable source of volunteers to help with special events, mail campaigns, or telemarketing. These groups will often be attracted to specific, time-limited volunteer activities in which their entire group can participate. Although your organization may not get the entire membership to continue as active volunteers after the activity is completed, you will often identify certain individuals within these groups who may want greater involvement.

Volunteer centers in your community, volunteer opportunities listed in newspapers, volunteer programs on high school or college campuses (where students are often required to perform volunteer community service as a graduation requirement), or individuals looking for development or marketing career experience are all excellent human resources for your organization.

Don't forget that volunteers are your best recruiters. Recruit and train your best volunteers to chair development activities such as special events or the annual campaign and then encourage them to recruit their own committee members. This often brings greater cohesiveness to a working committee. Often, friends and co-workers who know the chairperson enjoy working together.

Remember, you can't do it all! Use the talent, energy, and personal contacts of others to build your volunteer program. You may also choose a talented and committed volunteer to run the department's volunteer program.

A Volunteer's Expectations

A job description should be developed for each volunteer position, listing the main duties and responsibilities, time requirements, and reporting procedures. Several volunteers may share the same job description, (for example, a telemarketing position), but every volunteer recruit should be given a clear, written, job description.

Case Example

In order to find volunteers for a special event, the Ronald McDonald House of Minneapolis-St. Paul placed a brief job description in the volunteer opportunity column in the local paper. More than 60 people responded. After interviewing each volunteer prospect, the organization selected 45 volunteers to plan and implement its first-time celebrity golf tournament.

If volunteers lead the fund raising effort for your organization, you should set clear expectations of the staff support available to them and reach agreement on the division of responsibilities.

Volunteers should receive adequate training and a good orientation to the mission, programs, and services of your organization. Volunteers become an extension of your organization in the community and thus should be well versed in the workings of the organization.

Many organizations have adopted a Volunteer Bill of Rights to clarify volunteer expectations (see Illustration 2.) Such a statement can be included with a volunteer application or presented as an integral part of volunteer orientation.

Volunteer Responsibilities

Volunteers and staff work best together when there are clear expectations for volunteers. Before a volunteer begins serving your organization it is very important to have roles and responsibilities clearly understood by all parties. This will provide a more satisfying experience for the volunteer and improved results for your marketing program.

A Statement of Volunteer Responsibilities such as the one shown in Illustration 3, will help you to provide a clear and consistent message to all volunteers. It will also help the volunteer to meet reasonable expectations.

Case Example

The University of Minnesota's Carlson School of Management offers 28 internship teams each year to corporations and nonprofit organizations in the Minneapolis-St. Paul area. Each team of Master's Degree candidates works on a specific problem or project during a full semester and averages 20 hours of work for each of the 13 weeks. The school's team approach offers the host organization a broad range of skills and interests by each of the student interns, and a wide range of faculty resources to support the students in their research, project development, and final report. The cost for the internship team is based on a sliding fee scale, making it very affordable for nearly all nonprofit organizations.

Illustration 3: Volunteer Responsibilities

1. To make clear during the initial interview, your interests, skills, expectations, preferences, and availability.

2. To be aware of the general purpose of the agency and what is expected of you before accepting the assignment.

3. To accept the assignment with the intention of following through in a dependable manner, and to seek the assistance of your supervisor when needed.

4. To adhere to the policies and procedures established by the agency.

5. To notify your supervisor of necessary absences as much in advance as possible.

6. To participate in any training required by the agency.

7. To consult with your volunteer supervisor before accepting any new responsibilities.

8. To respect the confidentiality of agency and/or client information.

9. To discuss with your supervisor your satisfactions, dissatisfactions, and suggestions for upgrading or changing your assignment.

10. To be willing to respect the competencies of others and work as part of a team with all staff and other volunteers.

11. To share any notable medical or physical concerns.

Internships

Internships are wonderful opportunities for you to locate individuals with special skills or interests. Interns can assist you in many ways. For example, an intern may develop a concept and plan for a major fund raising event, conduct extensive prospect research, analyze a public relations program, survey donors about their perceptions of the effectiveness of your organization's programs and services, design policies and procedures for your marketing and development program, or initiate a cause-related marketing venture.

Internships may be offered to high school or college students or to professionals seeking to broaden their experience as part of a career change.

Interns will usually work with you for several weeks or several months, depending on the individual's school or work schedule. They may work part time or full time.

Some interns desire some form of stipend or financial compensation. Yet, there are others that desire only a meaningful work or career experience.

Many interns want to earn college credits. Therefore, they must have a measurable product to share at the end of their experience. They may be required to write a term paper, produce a report, or develop a plan. As the intern's supervisor, you may need to provide an evaluation of the intern's work.

Similar to volunteers and staff, the intern should have clear and measurable goals and objectives. In this manner, expectations are more likely to be fulfilled. The most important requirement is that the intern have a clearly defined job description.

If you wish to recruit an intern you should contact local colleges, business schools, and universities. Career placement agencies, voluntary service organizations, and corporate outplacement programs may also be excellent sources.

How to Recruit Valuable Board Members

One of the most important resources for the development program is the board of directors and its associated working and standing committees. You can ensure that you have a steady source of committed and talented volunteers by playing a strong role in identifying and nominating individuals to serve on board and committee positions.

Begin this task by identifying the skills and influence areas that are needed. For example, you may wish to recruit a vice president of marketing from a local corporation. This individual could not only assist you with marketing functions, but may also be able to help you secure additional in-kind or financial resources from his or her company. Ideally, the individuals must be willing to contribute their own time, talent, and financial resources to the organization.

Make the nominating and recruitment process part of your job description. You can do this by offering to serve as a member of the nominating committee of the board. Or, regularly provide names of candidates to your executive director or the board chair for consideration and recruitment.

Collaborations That Enlarge Your Possibilities

Collaboration can be a very effective means to achieve a goal when you would not otherwise have the human or financial resources to succeed on your own.

For example, which is better: to keep all of the proceeds of a small event or share the larger proceeds of a large event? Collaborating with other organizations can help you to expand your revenues and also reduce the financial risks of completely underwriting a special event.

Case Example

Children's Cancer Research Fund (CCRF) in Minneapolis, Minnesota, and two other small health service organizations were invited to participate in the grand opening of an upscale shopping mall. Each organization invited its donors and volunteers to attend the benefit event, which included food, drink, musical performances, and a silent auction. Each business at the mall donated an item for the silent auction.

A steering committee, consisting of representatives from each agency and the mall marketing staff, implemented the event. The revenue-sharing formula was as follows: each ticket buyer had the option of checking on the ticket which of the three charities would receive the proceeds. If ticket buyers did not select a charity, then their proceeds were divided equally among the three charities.

The event was a huge success. It brought an upscale audience to the mall opening, individuals had fun, and each charity expanded its visibility, and received close to $10,000 in proceeds.

Consider these examples:

- Two health-related agencies join together for a health expo.

- Area youth groups join forces to sponsor a fun run to increase revenues.

- Local schools jointly launch a career day for students and parents.

A collaborative effort may also be very attractive to corporate sponsors who are experiencing donor fatigue due to the numerous sponsorship requests they receive. Businesses often enjoy the opportunity to sponsor an event that will benefit several charitable organizations at a single time.

By collaborating with other agencies you can also reach a larger audience at an event because you can invite the volunteers and donors of all agencies involved.

The important point to consider when planning a collaborative effort is to clearly define each agency's roles and responsibilities and to agree upon a clear formula for dividing receipts. One agency may be responsible for invitations. Another may handle all of the logistics, and another may implement the day's activities. In other cases, all participating groups may try to share responsibilities equally. In many instances it may work best to have one organization take responsibility for organizing the entire event.

Formulas for sharing proceeds depend on work load; they may be shared equally, determined by a ratio of the number of volunteers who staff the event, or based on an agreed-upon percentage that is determined by how much work the organization performs.

The "Tom Sawyer" Approach

In order to be successful in your one-person shop, you must be able to get others to work with you. You must become like Tom Sawyer. Tom Sawyer had the unique ability to get others excited about his work. Often they were so excited that they actually paid him for the sheer privilege of participating. You can practice "Tom Sawyer" fund raising by getting others to help you with your development activities.

You can get corporations to sponsor your events, underwrite the costs of your publications, and even host your donor and volunteer recognition events. Although it may take extra time and effort to establish these relationships, the long-term benefits to your organization can be significant.

There are many individuals, organiza-

Collaboration can be a very effective means to achieve a goal when you would not otherwise have the human or financial resources to succeed on your own.

tions, and businesses in your community that want the opportunity to support an organization that provides valuable services to the community.

Like Tom Sawyer, it is your responsibility as a development professional to get others excited about taking part in a special project that is too difficult for a single individual.

A successful Tom Sawyer fund raiser also knows how to identify and go after the money that is out there looking for you.

A successful Tom Sawyer fund raiser also knows how to identify and go after the money that is out there looking for *you.* There are many organizations, businesses, schools, and churches in our communities that are constantly raising money to benefit charities. However, these groups often do not know where their funds will be directed each year.

For example, fraternal organizations, VFW and American Legion Posts, Rotary, Jaycees and Kiwanis Clubs, Junior Leagues, Knights of Columbus, and Haddassah are just some of the organizations involved in fund raising projects to benefit charity. In addition to the money they raise for specific charities and projects, they often have discretionary funds.

In addition, sports teams, school groups, fraternities and sororities, churches and synagogues also raise charitable dollars for nonprofit organizations.

Don't overlook some of the largest and most successful events in your community. Many change their beneficiaries from year to year. National organization events such as the NFL (National Football League)Alumni Association's annual banquet in each NFL community and the Hyatt Regency's "World's Largest Office Party," held in communities throughout the country, raise thousands of dollars for area charities. In addition to revenue, these events provide increased visibility for local organizations.

Also, don't assume that just because a sponsor has supported a certain charity for many years that it will continue to do so. From time to time many organizations and businesses look for new opportunities to support other worthwhile causes. If you position your organization to be in the right place at the right time, the benefits of the event may be directed your way.

By increasing the visibility of your organization, networking with community event sponsors, and enlisting the support of volunteers and donors to advocate on behalf of your organization, community benefit events may become integral to your development program.

Professional Associations

Membership in professional development associations such as the National Society of Fund Raising Executives (NSFRE) or the Council for Advancement and Support of Education (CASE) provide an invaluable resource to your small development shop. By participating in professional conferences, seminars, and meetings, you can hone your skills and enhance your knowledge by sharing practical experiences with other professionals.

Professional memberships also help you to develop a network of highly qualified development professionals whose experience and talent can be drawn upon when needed. This network may also be an important resource to you when advancing your career and pursuing new employment opportunities.

Review Checklist

√ Have you developed priorities for the goals and objectives within your development plan?

√ Have key management staff, volunteers, and advisors been involved in setting realistic expectations?

√ Do you recruit and train volunteers for your development program?

√ Is everyone connected to your organization involved in the development effort: volunteers, donors, staff, and board?

√ Are you involved in recruitment and training of board members?

√ Are you incorporating a Tom Sawyer approach to fund raising?

Conclusion

Identifying and involving the human resources in your community is perhaps the most important and cost-effective strategy to strengthen your development program. Effective fund raising is a team effort that enables you to achieve your goals through the involvement and support of others. Remember, you can't do it alone! You need to offer others -- staff, volunteers, interns, and collaborating nonprofit organizations -- the opportunity to share in your organization's mission. Help them to experience the joy of philanthropy.

RESEARCH

CHAPTER

2

- ■ *Surveys*
- ■ *Focus Groups*
- ■ *Cost-Effective Prospecting Techniques*
- ■ *Prospect Research by Computer*

Introduction

Market research is an integral part of any successful development program. Who are your donors and members? What motivates their giving and participation? What keeps them interested in your mission? How do they like to be acknowledged and recognized? These are all important questions you need to answer when developing your goals and strategies. You also need to research the wider audience of donor prospects to determine what approaches will be most appealing to them and how best to involve them in your organization. Even a small development shop can be very successful in conducting market research. This chapter will provide many effective and cost efficient ideas to strengthen your capabilities, including use of the latest technological advances pertaining to development.

Developing a Donor Profile: Clues and Techniques

Information such as a donor's age, marital status, gender, education, presence and age of children, and estimated income are essential in order to develop personalized cultivation and solicitation strategies. Although the following methods are not fail-safe, when used in combination, they provide valuable, detailed information about your donors.

Telephone Surveys

Telephone calls to thank key donors may generate a wealth of information. Consider this script: "I just opened your contribution envelope and was so excited to receive your gift that I wanted to call and just say thank you. Your gift will make a tremendous difference to the people we serve and it is greatly appreciated." In the course of this brief conversation with the donor, staff or volunteers may discover how the donor became involved with your organization, how his or her family may have benefited from your programs or services. The donor might also indicate an interest in providing additional support to your organization ("I may not have told you before but I have listed your organization in my will.") A positive response to a call may provide you with an opportunity to arrange for an in-person visit with a donor or member.

More extensive telephone surveys can also be conducted with donors or members. You may query them regarding the quality of your current programs, or get their opinion on a proposed new service. You may also ask questions about how the organization is perceived by the donor or member. Further, you may want to determine if the donor would utilize options such as electronic fund transfers or credit cards. Finally, in telephone interviews and written surveys, you may ask the donor or member if they would consider participating in a focus group.

Written Surveys

Written surveys are appropriate when you have a limited budget or are unable to reach the donor by other methods. Although this method does not provide in-depth information, if you have some specific ideas or questions that you would like to test, you can obtain some valuable information. Surveys can be mailed

separately or included in newsletters or annual reports. They may be used to ask basic questions regarding how the donor perceives your agency's operation or what programs and services most inspire the donor's giving.

Mini-surveys may also be used, consisting of one or two questions included in each newsletter or on a donor response card. Ask donors to identify the most pressing issues in your community, whether they would like to learn about volunteer opportunities, or if they would like to receive information on planned giving. In this manner you can begin to develop a more complete picture of their feelings, beliefs, and needs.

Remember that you must send many written surveys because the response ratio is often only 20%-50%. To encourage a higher response rate, incentives may be used. You may wish to enclose a dollar bill, a small premium, or an invitation to a special event.

Focus Groups

Focus groups provide more qualitative information than written surveys. In the focus group setting you can demonstrate a product, service, or activity. As well, you can gauge the emotional intensity of the participant's reactions. Participants may even provide solutions to problems when they are asked to consider creative

It is often said that if you ask donors for money, they will give you advice. But if you ask donors for advice, they will give you money.

15

options. Often focus groups provide rich data, including information or ideas that you may not have considered. One disadvantage of focus groups, however, is that they represent the ideas of only a select few. Thus, you may wish to compile data from several focus groups, and use this information, along with other data, to feed your evaluative thinking.

A professionally-directed focus group may take place in a special room where representatives of your board and/or management team can sit behind a two-way mirror to hear the discussion and record the comments of the participants. Participants are often not initially aware of who is sponsoring the focus group. This often creates a more open discussion by the attendees. The focus group leader, through a series of well-designed questions, will help focus the discussion on issues of interest to your organization.

If your organization is in a community where such professional services are not available or your budget is limited, you can conduct your own focus groups. First, randomly select a cross section of your target audience, enough so that you can be assured of at least five participants. A larger group of up to 15 participants is manageable, but may present difficulties for the novice facilitator. Also, try to organize a group that is as homogenous as possible. Consider whether participants will feel comfortably answering key questions with others in the group.

Allow at least 60-90 minutes for discussion. You also may wish to provide incentives for participation, such as food and small prizes. These are often donated by small businesses. A volunteer who is not well known to the audience may be an effective discussion leader. When a member of your organization is not serving as the focus group facilitator, you may receive more candid responses from participants.

You can direct audience discussion to several topics: ask participants about how they perceive your strongest competitors, how they perceive your organization, what motivates them to give to your organization, how they can become more involved with your programs and services, and what they anticipate for future needs. As well, you may want to ask them about specific products or services and how they can be improved.

Focus groups are an excellent tool to assist you in improving member and client relationships. The information you receive will result in the development of more appropriate services and products as well as improved results.

Prospect Research on a Shoestring Budget

In addition to the more standard research techniques mentioned earlier in this chapter, there are a number of other methods and ideas to help you identify and secure information about donors and prospects. Fund raising professionals refer to this process as "prospecting." These methods will enable you to identify potential donors, to locate information about their giving habits, place of business, financial worth, and to secure other public information that will help you shape your fund raising approach.

Detective Work with Envelopes and Checks

The donor envelope and check can provide some indications of key donor contacts within families. For example, although a married couple may be listed as donors on your records, the check may be consistently signed by only the wife or the husband. This is usually a good indication of who is responsible for sending the gift. Your cultivation efforts should be directed to this key family contact.

Checks received from your donors with very high check numbers may indicate that the donor is older and has used the account for many years, while checks with lower numbers may indicate a younger donor. A shaky signature on a check may identify an elderly donor. The return address on the envelope or check may also help you identify the donor within the family who is mailing the contribution. Specialty checks or return address labels may indicate special causes or interests the donor is helping to promote (i.e., checks promoting the environment, or labels with the logo of a local university).

CD-Rom Databases

Modern computers and other database services now allow you to gather information on a specific individual or company. This research is limited only by your ability to access and navigate these databases. If your budget does not include these services, consider accessing them at your local library.

Your local reference library may have one or more computers stocked with databases of various types. These include programs such as LEXUS, NEXUS, INFOTRAC, magazine article summaries and local newspapers.

Better yet, recruit volunteers or interns with computer skills, provide them with the specifics as to what information you are looking for, and allow them to conduct your donor research.

Organization Annual Reports

The annual reports of competing organizations can provide a treasure chest of prospect names for cultivation and solicitation. These publications list names of people who are interested in missions similar to yours, have the financial means to make a gift, and are obviously charitably inclined. In addition, gift levels listed in these reports will also help you determine an appropriate level of support to suggest to these new donor prospects. These reports can be obtained by calling an agency and asking for a copy, stopping by the office of a charitable organization to pick up a report, or using the resources of your local library, which most likely maintains files of newsclippings and annual reports of area organizations.

Form 990s

The Internal Revenue Service requires that nonprofit organizations raising more than $100,000 a year file a Form 990 with the IRS and with State Attorney General's office. These forms may also provide an excellent source of donor prospect names. Although the form filed with the IRS is confidential, the copy filed with the state is available to the general public in some states. Major donors' names, addresses, and amounts of gifts are often included in these reports.

You may wish to check with your State Attorney General's office to see if these reports are available for viewing or copying.

Special Event Programs

Those printed programs that people often leave behind on the dinner table or theater seat at special fund raising benefits can also be an important resource for names of corporations, foundations, and individuals who support organizations and missions similar to yours. Lists of key sponsors and patrons in these programs are invaluable leads on new donor prospects for your cause. Organizations may be willing to share their event programs with you. Another alternative is to ask donors and volunteers from your organization to secure copies of programs.

Corporate and Foundation Annual Reports

Most corporations and foundations provide their annual reports upon request. In addition to being easily attainable, these reports often list the names of the charitable causes that the corporation or foundation supports. Annual reports also describe the types of programs or projects with which they have been involved and the grant amounts given.

Newspapers: Business Section

Your metropolitan newspaper or local business newspaper will provide ample information about companies in your area. Note any mergers, acquisitions, quarterly earnings, or stock purchases. This information indicates the financial health of a company. Companies with high growth rates may be good prospects. Information about major foundations and nonprofit organizations may be listed here as well. Articles announcing promotions or hiring of key staff will keep you abreast of whom to contact, along with key biographical information, such as the individual's former place of employment, community affiliations, or experiences that have shaped his or her life.

Donor Plaques and Donor Walls

A visit to the lobbies of other non-profit organizations may also provide an abundance of names for your prospect list. Donor walls and plaques in museums, theaters, schools, churches, hospitals, and social service agencies can give you the key names and gift levels of donors in your community that you can pursue for support of your organization's programs and services.

Prospect Rating

Prospect rating is important for all development programs. It allows you to gather information about your donors, prospects, and members. This information will help you to rate their ability to give or increase their level of participation.

Some organizations employ the assistance of professional development consulting firms. They can rate your donor prospects through computerized analysis and compilation of information contained within public documents and a variety of other sources. They determine prospects' net worth through real estate and stock holdings, salary and benefit levels, education, family composition, memberships in organizations, service on boards of directors, involvement with nonprofit organizations, level of charitable giving, and propensity to give additional gifts to other charities.

This information is valuable but may be beyond the financial means of your organization. Still, even the smallest development shop can implement a low-cost prospect rating process that will strengthen its development efforts.

Networking

Developing, cultivating, and gathering information from a network of friends, professional associates, business and nonprofit leaders, and key community volunteers can provide invaluable information for your prospecting program.

Individuals who know important contributors in your community may help you learn more about the background, families, education, work, and social interests of your donor

There are many prospect-rating methods that provide an opportunity for you to gather information

prospects. Key community volunteers and donors may assist you in identifying prospects' charitable interests. As well, your professional development associates may share information that enables you to determine prospective donors' propensity for giving and the best cultivation and solicitation approaches to undertake.

In addition, working with attorneys, estate and financial planners, CPAs, insurance brokers, realtors, and bank trust officers can not only uncover new donor treasures but also allow "Tom Sawyer" fund raising to work for you once again. Friends in your professional network may introduce significant donor prospects to your organization's mission and important work. These professionals may have clients who wish to make charitable gifts directed to your organization as part of their financial and estate planning. Including professionals in your prospecting program will enhance the capabilities of your small development shop.

Prospect Research Committees

Prospect rating can be as simple as having a few key staff, donors, and volunteers review the donor list of your organization. They will note personal relationships or associations with donors and provide information about the donors' careers, families, involvement with other charitable organizations, financial ability to give, giving history, likelihood of giving, and suggestions for how you can cultivate the donors' interests. Another excellent method used to gather information and to rank your donor prospects is by using the expertise of several individuals working on a prospect research committee. For example, bankers and realtors may know of the assets or holdings of an individual or of other interests in the community. This information would help you to establish appropriate gift "asks," encouraging higher levels of giving when appropriate.

These individuals might be those same professionals listed earlier in the preceding paragraph on networking. Or, they might be former board members or volunteers who seem to have many friends and contacts.

Observe the Prospect Rating Form that appears in Illustration 4. This form allows you to consider several aspects of an individual's or corporation's involvement. Each prospect or donor would be rated on a scale of 1-5 for each category.

Organizational data is the typical source for much of this information, to be shared with your prospecting committee.

Participants must know that this information will be kept confidential, to be used only by your staff or campaign solicitors.

Illustration 4; Prospect Rating Form

Prospect Rating Form

Allot points from 0-5, depending on degree of involvement

Use notes as necessary

Name	Individual giving	Multiple gifts	Major gifts >250	Capital gifts	Volunteerism	Years involved	Special	Total

Although many development managers may already be aware of the print resources available, the most up-to-date version of these print resources can be accessed directly -- right on your own computer.

Additionally, you may discover that some of the members of your prospect research committee make excellent campaign solicitors because of their many contacts. Your committee is an ideal forum to begin to put together a solicitor's group, if the right candidates are available.

Discover the Prospect Researcher Hidden in Your Computer

Grant amounts are declining and your odds are decreasing. How do you maintain a leading edge? Many managers are doing just that through comprehensive research. Although many development managers may already be aware of the print resources available, the most up-to-date version of these print resources can be accessed directly — right on your own computer. Let's discuss just a few of the many options available.

When seeking funding for a project, most grant writers research several different funding options by reviewing corporate or foundation grantmaking guidelines or annual reports.

There are also many excellent sources to help you identify and research funders. The *Catalog of Federal Domestic Assistance* is the most comprehensive catalog available for federal funds. It presents the

programs of all federal agencies, including their requirements and points of contact. A computerized version, *Federal Access Programs Retrieval System*, is also available. With a personal computer and modem, you may access information, paying only nominal charges. For more information contact: (202) 453-4126.

Another method of accessing the *Federal Register* is to go to the web site for the U.S. Government Printing Office. This will alert you to the *Catalog of Federal Domestic Assistance.*

Other sources for government funds include the *State Register*, published once weekly, and the *Federal Register.* It is helpful to read the *Federal Register* with regularity. Frequently, sponsoring agencies will issue "Notices of Proposed Rulemaking" (NPR). In the NPR, public comment is invited to respond to a proposed "rule," or grant priority that will subsequently be issued. These comments are compiled, and six to nine months later a more complete request for proposals will be published, reflecting the comments and opinions of field professionals. Reading the NPRs will allow you to get a head start on developing your proposals.

ERIC, the world's largest education database, is another tool that will provide valuable information. ERIC's on-line services supply documentation about recent studies and findings related to education and human services. Like any reliable information source, ERIC is a good tool to use when grantseeking. Database information sources are often used to supply current and past research findings to help you document problem statements. Similarly, you may use these sources to validate your project method, identifying similar approaches or methods that have met with success.

A database available through Knight-Ridder Information system (formerly known as DIALOG) tracks the *Federal Register* (file 669). Updated weekly, this database, the *Federal Register Abstracts* (FRA) (file136), may be used individually, or can be accessed at your local foundation center or library (1-800-334-2564 is the toll-free phone number for Knight-Ridder Information).

FEDIX (Federal Information Exchange) provides on-line services about grants available from several major federal agencies, including the Department of Education, the Office of Scientific Research, the Department of Housing and Urban Development, Federal Aviation Administration, National Science Foundation, National Security Agency, Office of Naval Research, U.S. Agency for International Development, Department of Commerce, Department of Energy, and more. This is a free service that can be accessed with your personal computer and modem by calling 1-800-232-4879 or through the Internet. To access by Internet, simply log on to the local access, then type telnet address fedix.fie.com. Once you receive the prompt, type "fedix."

The Knight-Ridder Information Services database is usually available at major reference libraries. Or, you may call 1-800-334-2564 to access other important funder information. Equally important as locating funding sources is avoiding duplication of existing projects. FRIP (Federal Research in Progress) provides information about federally funded research projects in the physical and life sciences.

Corporate Giving Programs are detailed in the *Foundation Directory* (FD), whose printed form is compiled by the Foundation Center. The Foundation Center also publishes a user manual and thesaurus to show you how to retrieve facts quickly from the Foundation Center databases.

More recent listings of corporate grants and their amounts may be found in the *Foundation Grants Index* (FGI). This provides more detailed information than that given in the Foundation Directory, highlighting grant recipients, subject areas, date of awards, and geographic areas of interest.

Many grant writers are already familiar with *Source Book Profiles*, or *Foundation 1000*, as it is now called. While this book profiles major funders, the

National Data Book will highlight smaller funders, providing point of contact and basic grantmaking activities.

These files may be purchased individually, or they may be accessed through subscription to on-line vendors, such as *America Online, CompuServe, Microsoft Network,* and *Prodigy.*

Specific Fund Raising On-Line Services

Knight-Ridder Information has more than 400 databases with a vast array of information resources. In addition to the *Foundation Directory* (file 26) mentioned earlier which provides funding guidelines, you might try The Foundation Grants Index (file 27). Also try *Dun & Bradstreet Market Identifiers* (file 516), which lists marketing information on more than 10 million companies, *Standard & Poor's Register (file 526),* and *Marquis Who's Who Directories* (file 234).

Additional tools for researching individuals are available on Knight Ridder Information. The database ONESEARCH contains category files such as BIOGRAPH and PEOPLE which lists prominent men and women. Stock holdings are found in SEC Online information files 100 (Disclosure) and 540 (Disclosure/Spectrum Ownership).

Another valuable file for needs assessment work in the grants area is the *CompuServe* (GO DEMO-GRAPHICS) file. Here, information is given for any area in the U.S., including population, income, age and race of residents. This data is based on 1990 Census information and five-year forecasts. To get a list of other demographic databases available on *CompuServe* use the command: GO DEMOGRAPHICS ($50 yearly) Catalog (FAPRS).

Other services offered through *CompuServe* include Phone*File, a directory of approximately 85 million phone numbers for individuals that can be accessed by name with an address, surname with city or state, or surname with zip code or by phone number. Company information is available on Knowledge Index and IQUEST and *Standard & Poor's Register.*

ORYX Press offers a public and private grants database available on CD-Rom making it possible for you to search without communications software. This broad base of information is at your disposal to search on many topics and geographic areas.

Accessing this information on your personal computer can be time-consuming, due to the massive amounts of data, subheads, and categories that you must bypass before reaching your target destination. This is a skill that requires practice and knowledge of the sources in question. If your time is limited, you may wish to consider subscribing to a research service that will complete your search.

One such source is the National Grantseekers Institute. They can be reached by calling 1-800-655-5597. For an annual fee of $299, they will perform 24 searches during the year.

Review Checklist

√ Do you, on a regular basis, implement activities to determine the needs of your donors and key publics?

√ Do you rely upon an ongoing program of donor research, cultivation and recognition in order to secure, maintain, and upgrade donor involvement?

√ Is a prospect rating system being used by your organization to determine the giving potential of donors and donor prospects?

√ In what ways can database research assist your development program?

Conclusion

Research will help you determine how to spend your limited time, as well as how to effectively target your proposals and solicitation letters and other marketing communications. Although there are many more sophisticated tools available now for researching by computer, the majority of resources available can be found readily within your own working environment. Taking the time to use these valuable resources will significantly improve your fund raising and marketing capabilities.

Maintaining contact with donors and members is the key to raising money. In-person contact usually works best, but since every situation will not permit a personal contact, you, the development professional, should decide how to use your time and research resources to your best advantage.

TECHNOLOGY

CHAPTER

3

- ■ **Needs Assessment**
- ■ **Options for Organizations with Small Budgets**
- ■ **Customized or "Off the Shelf" Software**
- ■ **Improving Management with Technology**
- ■ **Should You Go On-line?**
- ■ **Cost-saving Multi-media**
- ■ **Communication Equipment**

Introduction

Organizations of all sizes are now preparing to enter the age of technology. In more ways than you can imagine, using computer software programs to track and manage your data will save you time and money. Without question, operating without technology may place an individual or organization at a considerable disadvantage. For this reason, an increasing number of nonprofit organizations are acquiring technology. As the price of computers, software, and hardware systems continues to decrease, these systems are coming within the price range of all types of users.

Moreover, many computer software programs are now available to meet your needs. These programs include accounting, budgeting, grants administration, mailing, marketing, gift and donor tracking, prospecting, and planned giving.

These technological solutions will help your organization to minimize expenses and staff time, as well as help you to access and manage critical data and information. Whether your budget is large or small, these technological advances are worth considering

This chapter will provide you with some basic information about how to get started and where to locate resources. It will also provide a review of the types of technologies available. As you read this chapter, it will be useful to remember that technology is changing so quickly that even as this book is printed, some of the following options may be obsolete, or replaced by better, more efficient options. Despite this limitation, you will benefit by considering what new technologies are available to meet your organizational needs.

Getting Started: Conduct a Needs Assessment

The first critical step in developing a technology plan is to determine your organizational needs. Your needs assessment should consider all administrative and management functions within the organization such as:

- Program planning and tracking;

- Donor tracking and management;

- Marketing research;

- Public relations/communications; and

- Financial management.

Once you have prioritized the areas and tasks that you wish to manage, you will be in a better position to recruit a technology professional or team of experts to help you evaluate various software programs and their respective support systems. Another option is to recruit a local computer consulting firm or corporation who may be willing to provide its staff.

When evaluating your options, you may also wish to consider:

- The organizational budget;

- The capabilities of your staff or volunteers;

- The capabilities of your existing software and hardware systems;

- The need for training and on-going support;

- The costs versus capabilities of various options.

If your organization has a collection of old computers along with a few newer models, you may wish to consider how to use the newer computers in a more effective configuration. This may include staggering work times or relocating equipment so that it may be used by more than one staff person.

Training and on-going support capabilities are critical to the adequate performance and maintenance of your

---

Case Example

In the January 1993 issue of *Nonprofit World*, Christian Homes, a licensed child placement service, discussed the benefits of their recent fund raising software program. Since they acquired the software, their pledge donations increased by 30 percent with a savings of $2,000 in clerical costs. Because the organization was now able to target selective groups of donors and analyze past appeals, they were able to raise the same amount of money at only 10 percent of the cost.

technology systems. If staff are unfamiliar with how to operate the technology, then they will be limited in their ability to maximize their potential.

One low-cost training option that is often overlooked is computer user's groups. User groups are informally organized groups of individuals who meet to discuss the use of a particular software program. User groups are the perfect place for you or your staff

---

Case Example

Like other social service organizations, the Urban Communities Association of Minneapolis (UCAM) needed a vehicle to track program enrollment. Unfortunately, the organization's computer systems were so outdated that some staff members had to bring more modern equipment from home in order to do simple word processing. Further, other staff members lacked the skills to operate computers and had to rely upon time-consuming manual systems.

Hodiak Development had been working with UCAM to secure grants for program and operating costs. Knowing that funders were increasingly interested in organizations that effectively tracked and evaluated their programs, Hodiak suggested that funders might also provide for equipment in order to complete such evaluations. Hodiak further suggested that UCAM target those funders who had already awarded management and capability improvement grants for nonprofit organizations.

A volunteer, a professional systems manager from a local corporation, helped the staff determine needs for hardware, software, and related equipment. This not only provided in-kind support for the project, but also let prospective funders know that the staff had thoroughly done their homework. A detailed needs assessment was prepared, showing the type of equipment, manufacturer, its costs, and the need and costs for training.

In the proposal, the needs assessment was intimately tied to a new evaluation and donor tracking system that would be put in place. Such systems, the proposal explained, would dramatically improve the organization's ability to monitor client progress and demographics, and help to maintain donor accounts. New equipment would significantly decrease staff time devoted to the present cumbersome tracking system. Moreover, new systems would improve client data privacy, an increasingly important need with the increased incidence of litigation. UCAM's proposal was accepted in full by a regional foundation.

to share ideas. Even with technical support available through the manufacturer, it often is necessary to troubleshoot smaller problems. A local computer publication may provide information about user groups. Or, call your local manufacturer sales representatives or local computer businesses that offer computer technical support or retail sales. They may know where local user groups operate. If you live in an area where no such groups exist, you may wish to start your own group.

Grants for Technology

Technology resources are often costly capital investments. For this reason, their cost can be hard to justify to board members and foundations. Nonetheless, organizations without access to technology often fall behind, or are likely to incur other costs that may exceed the original cost of equipment.

More and more funders are beginning to realize that organizations must have adequate technological resources. Hence, government, corporate, and foundation funders are likely prospects for a major technology grant. Developing a major grant, and a thorough development of a case for support that outlines what the proposed technologies will make possible, takes time. The case example on the preceding page describes how one organization met this

challenge and managed to acquire a new computer system.

Other technology projects have met with similar success from corporate, private, and/or government funders. These successful proposals have normally gone beyond a description of the need for updating equipment. They explain what the technology will help the organization to accomplish, particularly in the area of improved services, improved staff effectiveness, or increased cost savings.

More than ever, funders are hoping to maximize their investments. Funders interested in maximizing organizational capability or management effectiveness will often entertain such projects, but only if a comprehensive needs assessment (often with assistance from a professional) indicates that equipment purchase is the best viable option.

Other Options

In the near term, while you are waiting for major support, you may wish to consider some of the following options.

Donated Software

Many software retailers and manufacturers have programs to donate software to 501(c)3 organizations.

One low-cost training option that is often overlooked is computer user's groups.

Local corporations are also excellent resources. Many companies will auction items at low prices or donate goods to charitable organizations.

Gifts in Kind America
700 N. Fairfax St. # 300
Alexandria VA 22314
(Contact with a self-addressed, stamped envelope.)

All charities, except religious organizations, are eligible to receive free copies of software, with only a $25 handling charge. The types of software available may vary at the time of the request, but may include spreadsheet, word processing, graphics, and/or organizing programs.

CompuMentor
(415) 512-7784 (office)

This organization sells donated software to nonprofit groups for a minimal price.

East-West Education Development Foundation
(617) 542-1234 (office)
(617) 542-2345 (fax)

Located in Boston, this organization refurbishes computers for distribution to groups in 150 countries.

Global Recycling Network
(516) 286-5580 (office)
http://grn.com/grn/,e-mail to
grn@gm.com (web site)

This group offers a $30 monthly service that matches buyers and sellers of recyclable items. Users search by keyword for the name of the item and are alerted by e-mail when a match is found.

Nonprofit Computing
40 Wall Street, Suite 2124
New York NY 10005-1301
(212) 759-2368 (office)

This company was founded by an international banker and a business systems consultant to provide volunteer technical assistance and training to nonprofit organizations. They exchange information and donate equipment after the recipient's need analysis is completed.

National Cristina Foundation
591 East Putnam Ave.
Greenwich CT 06830
(800)-Cristina   (office)
(203) 622-6000 (office)
(203) 622-6270 (fax)

The National Cristina Foundation was originally founded to aid people with disabilities, at-risk students, and others with economic disadvantages in gaining access to an important training tool, the computer. Organizations are requested to complete the following information in the application: level of computer expertise, whether they have access to individuals who can install and/or repair older technology, whether training is available, and if they can arrange for pick-up when donations become available in their part of the country.

Should You Customize Your Software or Buy off the Shelf?

It's true that fund raising software programs are a costly investment. Often it may seem to be infinitely less expensive to use an existing relational database, such as Microsoft *Access* or another comparable program, and have a computer expert set up the database files. For organizations that want to implement simple file segmentation, with files of less than 3,000 names, operated by staff who are very knowledgeable in the database program, this may be suitable.

However, consider the following scenario. It is a distinct probability for those who decide to customize. As your need to segment, prepare, and report data files becomes more sophisticated, a problem develops in completing a program function. You are unable to find a solution. But who can you call for help? You must contact the original programmer, or someone

who knows the programmed language, to provide the "fix." Unfortunately, no two programmers ever develop a program in the same way. Such a system makes it very difficult to complete work in a timely fashion. And if your original programmer is no longer available, it may be extremely difficult for anyone else to update your program. If you decide that custom programming is your best option, then you should insist that your programmer develop some type of written documentation so that others can also understand the system.

This is why the "off the shelf" program has several advantages. Companies offering these designed and tested programs normally offer training at regularly scheduled times. They have technical support available and standardized methods for executing reports, queries and file preparation. They also usually have a written manual or training diskette. These are essential items when considering any software program.

Obtaining Computer Hardware at Low or No Cost

Many nonprofit organizations obtain computer equipment through contributions or at a minimal cost. When seeking computer hardware, it's important to remember to obtain the proper equipment necessary to run

Many nonprofit organizations successfully obtain computer equipment through contributions or at a minimal cost.

the computer software programs you have chosen. With the rapid changes taking place in computer technology it is very easy to find donors who will donate "computers" to your organization. However, it is extremely important to remember that you don't just need a "computer." You also need appropriate computer hardware including processors, monitors, modems, and printers that are in good working condition, all of which should meet your needs.

Effective use of your organization's wish list (see Chapter 8) will inform donors, volunteers, and businesses in your community of your specific needs. Corporations in the process of upgrading equipment or rightsizing their departments often decide to auction or donate leased or barely-used equipment when it no longer meets their needs.

Nonprofit organizations in your community who are upgrading their equipment may also be willing to donate their used equipment to your organization. In addition, they may be willing to refer you to other potential equipment donors.

Remember to be specific. Obtain the computer hardware you need. Don't become a dumping ground for outdated and useless equipment given by "generous" donors.

Should You Go On-line?

According to recent research, the primary users of the Internet are highly educated and make incomes of $80,000 or more. In coming years, however, it is anticipated that more and more users of all kinds will access the Internet. Therefore, it is a tool worth your consideration. A complete discussion of Internet use goes well beyond the scope of this book. Therefore, we will discuss some of its more pertinent highlights. If you desire more information, consult the section on "Further Resources" that appears at the end of this chapter.

Since the dawn of the Internet, more and more people have been communicating and accessing information in new, more efficient ways. An internet is a joining of two computers to form a *local area network*, or *internet*. The Internet (notice the capital "I") is the huge, overall combination of internets, or local area networks. It contains millions of individuals who are accessing data, programs, machines, and software programs. They operate locally and worldwide.

When you use the internet, or Internet, you establish a connection between your computer and a distant host. You, the recipient, or client, may use either the Mac or IBM computer platform. Host computers are generally the most powerful. Although both sides of the connection may operate on a simple microcomputer, or personal computer, host computers are generally larger because of the storage and processing requirements of managing large files.

Many nonprofit managers currently use on-line services. Among other benefits, these on-line services can provide you with up-to-date information related to your grantseeking. They will help you complete proposal research and provide information on various nonprofit organizations, businesses, and corporations.

Many nonprofit organizations also use on-line formats to promote their programs and services and to solicit financial support from a worldwide audience directly. Some transmit messages across the globe, saving costly transmission charges for faxes and long-distance phone.

Internet Resources

Today, there are many Internet sites that you may access for funding information. The advantage of the Internet is that you can receive this information immediately, rather than waiting for the request to leave the in-basket and post office. Future theorists contend that in the next ten years most funders will provide information in this manner, rather than through the more costly method of printing and mailing. A few foundations and government funders have already started this process:

- IBM (grant and equipment donation programs for education, environment and workforce development). At http://www.ibm.com/IBM/IBM gives/index.html.

- Westinghouse Foundation (supports projects in education, health and welfare, civic and social organizations in communities where it has facilities). At http://www.westinghouse.com/ca/ca_hp.htm.

- Most state and federal government funders have set up e-mail addresses that can be accessed on the Internet.

Education/Training/Information

The Internet will also provide you with access to other professionals through discussion groups known as Usenet groups. An example of a group that provides information on fund raising events, management, and programming is Usenet: soc.org.nonprofit.

The possibilities present in on-line services are immense. Such an asset requires preparation, however. Because on-line database services represent such a powerful array of information, accessing this information presents its own complexities. You may wish to take a class in operating on-line services, or read one of several guides that are available. A list appears at the end of this chapter.

Communications Equipment for On-line Services

Most personal computers are configured with a hard drive and a port that allows you to plug in a modem, a device that provides the telephone connection and file transfer capabilities needed for on-line services. When purchasing a modem, you may wish to consider BAUD rates, which is the rate at which the modem will transmit characters (letters and symbols) on-line. The actual character transmission rate is limited to the lowest BAUD rate of the modem at either end of the communications link. Therefore, before purchasing a modem, you may wish to find out the BAUD rate of your on-line service vendor. Modems can now be purchased for as little as $100.

To complete your on-line communications package you will also need a software communications program (such as *Pro-comm*) to complete the task.

Consider Cost

Preparing to go on-line can seem like an insurmountable hurdle, considering the vast array of services, hardware, and software options. Here are some things to consider before making a purchase:

How often will you use the system? Costs to consider include yearly subscription fees as well as hourly usage fees. Depending on the source, some files are more expensive to transfer than others.

How easy is the system to use? Does the service provide training, manuals, or other services to make services user-friendly?

Who else is using the service? If an organization wishes to communicate with educational agencies, then a service with many users from education would be an ideal choice.

Services To Meet Your Unique Needs

Large commercial vendors, such as America Online, CompuServe, Microsoft Network, or Prodigy, are perhaps most well known.

America Online: (212) 475-1001

America Online (AOL) now allows nonprofit organizations to list volunteer openings or other charity-related topics free of charge. A monthly fee of $25 enables an organization to be included in a database that lists basic contact information, mission, and three items or services they most need. Access.point, a New York-based company, sets up the new section. Contact James Clark, Access.point, 30 Irving Place, New York, NY 10003, (212) 475-1001 for more information.

In addition, AOL offers access to the Internet for individuals wishing to conduct prospect research. You may use documents and resources throughout the country. AOL offers a basic service or unlimited use of the Internet for a slightly higher monthly fee.

CompuServe: (800) 848-8199

If you feel that you have a product or service that would be of interest to CompuServe members, CompuServe encourages you to submit a proposal for consideration. You can obtain the form at http;/www. compuserve com. This form can be completed on-screen and transmitted back to the company on the Internet.

Prodigy: (800) 776-3449

Prodigy was the first plan that allowed you to be on-line and on the Internet at the same time.

Microsoft Network (MSN): *(800)123-4567*

Microsoft Network is expanding its services. They can also be reached at http:/www.microsoft.com.

Other options are also available to nonprofit organizations.

Institute for Global Communications

The Institute for Global Communications, a nonprofit organization originated by grants from several foundations, provides a variety of telecommunication services, including electronic mail, conferences, database research, publishing, access to the Internet, and other special programs. Depending on your organization's needs, subscribing to the Institute's services may be more cost-effective than subscribing to commercial computer communications services.

On-line services can provide current information for grants, as well as informtion pertinent to prospect research.

35

World Wide Web Home Page

The World Wide Web (WWW) is the newest and most significant Internet development. WWW is a vehicle through which you can market information about your organization. Providing your own WWW Home Page (or server) is similar to providing an advertisement that is available 24 hours a day. If a user is interested in more information, they need only to leave their electronic mail number in your home page mailbox. Some home pages receive hundreds of calls each day.

Many vendors, paid and free, are now setting up home pages for nonprofit organizations. You may wish to contact your local newspaper, television station, or telephone company to see if they provide such a service. Alternatively, you could contact a local corporation to see if they might provide their computer staff to help you design your organization's home page.

The requirements to set up and maintain a WWW home page may include:

■ A modem and computer as mentioned in this chapter under Communication Equipment for On-line Services;

■ A minimal set-up fee for a graphic artist to design the home page;

■ Training for your staff on Internet access;

■ Staff time for responding to requests for information;

■ Staff time to update and maintain your home page;

■ Staff training on how to do WWW updating;

■ Costs of space: usually up to five megabytes are allowed, without extra charges for the home page.

The Internet has yet to prove itself as a fund raising vehicle. Nonetheless, it does provide a means for you to build your database, provide public information, and reach special target audiences who are Internet users.

Illustration 5-1: ARC Home Page

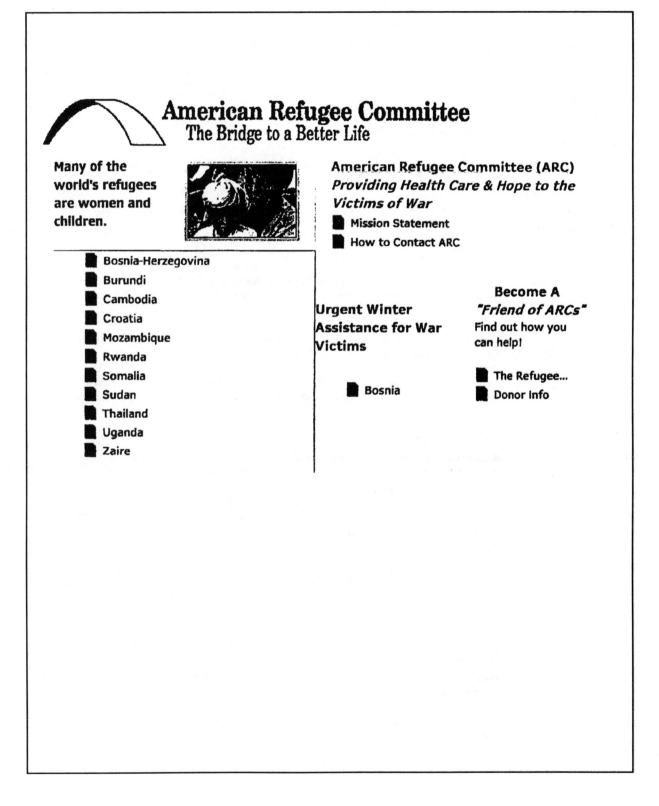

Illustration 5-1: ARC Home Page, page 2

American Refugee Committee

Ways You Can Help Refugees
Become a "Friend of ARC"   0 00 12:00am

Call 1-800-329-4447 to help make a difference in the world.

Let us know what you think!

Write ARC at: ARC@Ichange.com

Give the Gift of Life and Hope

There are many ways to make a gift to support the work of the American Refugee Committee in refugee sites throughout the world.

Cash Gifts
A check written to the American Refugee Committee will be used to bring medical care and health care training to refugees where the need is greatest. A gift charged through your VISA or Mastercard is also an easy means to make a gift that will have a direct impact on peoples' lives.

Donors wishing to become monthly or quarterly contributors may notify the ARC office and have timely reminders and donor envelopes mailed to them.

Your employer may match your gift. Many companies match their employees gifts to charitable organizations. Consult your personnel office; you may be able to double or triple your gift by using your employer's matching gift program.

Wills and Bequests
A gift in support of the American Refugee Committee through your will may have substantial tax benefits for you and your heirs and serve as a lasting tribute to your support of the work of ARC. Gifts specified in your will may include cash, securities, real estate, artwork and other types of personal property. ARC always appreciates being notified that the organization has been named in your will so that your gift can be acknowledged and, if desired, you can be recognized for your contribution during your life.

Life Insurance
Life insurance can also be used as a gift by making the American Refugee Committee the owner and beneficiary of your policy. The tax benefits vary according to whether it is a paid up policy or one on which you are still paying the premiums.

Charitable Trusts
There are many other ways to make a gift, some of which may bring you income during your lifetime, reduce your income taxes and estate taxes, and support the organization after your death. These include the creation of trusts such as a charitable remainder trust, charitable gift annuity, and the charitable lead trust.

For further information regarding gift opportunities with the American Refugee Committee, please call Michael Henley, Director of Development and Public Affairs at (612) 872-7060.

How to Create a Successful Web Site or Home Page

Easy navigation, attractive graphics, and compelling interaction are the keys to a successful home page. This means that graphics should be small and easy for viewers to access. One option is to use only text on your home page, allowing the viewer to access information quickly, without graphics. Frequent updates of your site will also encourage users to connect often, looking for more valuable information. Free demos, contests, or information are always a plus. You also may want to consider a donor-feedback line to gather valuable information for planning. Remember always to protect your donor's privacy by not requesting too much personal information. Allowing a donor to maintain anonymity is important to survey accuracy.

If you're still not quite sure how to develop your own site, a number of vendors now offer software that can do it for you. Microsoft's *Front Page*™ is a Web editor that you can use without any prior Web programming language, called HTML. It works like a simple word processor. This product was released in 1996. *Front Page* ™ also includes a program to manage a Web site. Other vendors, such as Adobe and Incontext, are also developing similar software for release in the near future.

Users will be delighted if they can also access other information while connecting with your site. Encourage interconnectivity by providing links to other Web sites that relate to yours. If you can generate a relationship with another organization or business, then perhaps a mutual link can be set up to provide more traffic.

Remember that an unresponsive or unreliable Web site can actually be a detriment to your organization. Therefore, make sure that you devote adequate resources to managing your site, so that respondents can get answers to their questions. Remember that the Web works 24 hours a day, so it is a powerful tool for allowing others to access your organization. You may need to consult occasionally with a Web technician to get answers to questions or to correct problem areas. Your biggest expense, however, will be for staff who are responsible for managing the site. Some sites require up to one full-time staff person to manage a large, multifaceted site.

Cost-Saving Multimedia Advances

More and more organizations are seeking new ways to improve the quality of their communication with their publics. A variety of new communication methods will assist you in this process. Although unheard of 20 years ago, today more than half of all Americans own and regularly operate a VCR. CD-Rom units now transfer large amounts of information via sound bytes. These and other equally exciting new communication venues will continue to offer new opportunities.

Interactive Television

The Nonprofit Organizations' New Media Center, a program of the Interactive Television Association, has published *Questions and Answers About Interactive Television*, a primer for nonprofit organizations that explains the pros and cons of interactive television. It is available free from:

Nonprofit Organizations' New
Media Center
1030 Fifteenth St./ M/W/ # 1053
Washington DC 20005
(202) 408-0008 (office)
(202) 408-0111 (fax)

OCR Scanners

OCR, optical character reading, scanners are the basis for bar-coding applications. Since their appearance on the market a few years ago, many uses for this technology have developed. OCR scanners can be used to scan text on a page for input directly into a computer word-processing program. Such a technique is extremely useful in minimizing staff time for the re-typing of documents that cannot be transmitted by computer diskette or modem. Offices that routinely manage documents acquired from others can save on courier fees and retyping charges by using an OCR scanner. Some OCR scanners include a computer software program to facilitate input directly into your word-processing program. Other less costly models may require you to "piece" documents together.

Digital Cameras

Just a few years ago, digital cameras came on the market. Today, these handy cameras enable you to take many photos, in color or black and white, and *digitize* them for use with your computer, eliminating the costs of film development or scanning. Digitizing refers to the process of transmitting bits of graphic information so it can be read by a computer. Digital cameras can be purchased for as little as $200 for a black-and-white version, capable of transmitting photos at a resolution of 300 dots per inch. This is suitable for newsletter-quality photos or for placement into video tapes as still frames. If you do a lot of photography and wish to eliminate the additional steps and costs of scanning and film development, a digital camera may be worth considering. Rent one from a local supplier to see what they can do for you.

Compact Disc Interactive (CDI) Technology

It is often difficult for a small development staff with a limited budget to meet and cultivate donors who live outside of their community. Imagine the benefit of mailing a small compact disc to distant donors that allows them to select specific information about your organization. At their own convenience, donors could receive an update on your latest program developments by viewing a video, seeing and hearing testimonials from program participants, viewing graphs of program outcomes, reviewing your budget and income growth, and looking at future planning documents.

Compact disc interactive (CDI) technology offers the benefit of audio, video, and graphic presentations all within one system. It presents audiovisual information in a format that allows individuals to control what they view, hear, and read. The result is that they stay interested longer, pay more attention, and learn more.

CDI provides a more engaging alternative for organizations now using videotape, film, audiotapes, slides, and/or computers. It presents unique opportunities to train volunteers, inform the public of programs and services, cultivate prospects, and bring exciting and graphic images of your organization to donors and members. It also provides a method to reach large numbers of individuals.

Another advantage is that no technical skills are required to operate a CDI system. As easy as a video game, CDI allows viewers to interact with visuals, audio, text, graphics, and animation. It can even be multilingual. CDI's multi-track audio recording capability lets you run several language tracks on the same disc at the same time. The CDI disc will also play on any CDI player worldwide.

One limitation of CDI is that most people do not have CDI equipment and may not be familiar with the technology. However, as the market expands for CDI technology, it will become a more viable alternative for nonprofit organizations to use in promoting their programs and services.

Another consideration is that the original development of CDI technology may be expensive. Despite this liability, there are a number of opportunities that you can consider. Perhaps a vendor in your area is hoping to showcase this technology to a new, wider audience and would offer to donate the service. Or, you can minimize your costs by providing the script, photography, or still frames, and using a vendor only to assemble the project. Fortunately, once the program has been developed into CD-Rom format, reproduction is minimal ($1.00 to $2.00 per copy, depending on quantity.)

Further Resources:

Proposal Planning and Writing. Lynn E. Miner and Jerry Griffith. ORYX Press,1993.

The Internet Yellow Pages. Harley Hahn and Rick Stout. Osborne McGraw-Hill, (510) 549-6600.

The Windows Internet Tour Guide. Michel Fraase. Ventana Press. (800) 743-5369.

The Mac Internet Tour Guide. Michael Fraase. Ventana Press. (800) 743-5369.

Inside CompuServe. Richard Wagner. New Riders/Macmillan Computer Publishing. (800) 428-5331.

Using America On-line. Steinberg & Stroud. Que/Macmillan Computer Publishing, (800) 428-5331.

Windows Shareware 500. John Hedtke. Ventana Press. (800) 743-5369.

Mac Shareware 500. Ruffin Prevost & Rob Terrell. Ventana Press. (800) 743-5369.

On-line Systems for Nonprofits. Compumentor. 89 Stillman Street. San Francisco, 94107: (415) 512-7784.

Review Checklist

√ Has your organization secured the assistance of technology and office systems personnel in order to conduct a needs assessment?

√ Has your organization conducted a needs assessment to determine if adequate technologies and office systems are in place for maximum efficiencies?

√ If budgets are limited, has your organization set in place a technology plan that includes securing the equipment, training, and resources necessary? Does it include a time line for implementation? This may include a five-year plan for securing grants or donated equipment.

√ To what extent is existing technology being used to improve effectiveness? To what extent can your organization utilize outside resources to provide these services and improve cost effectiveness?

Although this question may apply to communications of all kinds, it should specifically be considered in relationship to the ongoing management of the donor or client database, mail-management systems, and donor research databases.

Conclusion

Increased information access through technology will more and more become the manager's key organizational tool. Technology will facilitate better decision-making and provide vehicles for better, more refined communications with key constituencies. Given these advantages, it behooves managers to stay abreast of the breakthroughs in technology.

PLANNING : THE KEY TO SUCCESS

CHAPTER

4

- ■ **The Strategic Plan**
- ■ **Mission Statement**
- ■ **The SWOT Analysis**
- ■ **The Competitor Analysis**
- ■ **Service Configuration Matrix**
- ■ **Constituency Circle**
- ■ **Evaluation**

Introduction

How many development professionals get too busy to plan? It's more common than you might imagine. Yet, planning is the single most important ingredient for the success of your organization. Planning enables a manager to sort priorities, to take stock of past successes and shortcomings, and to invest resources in the most promising alternatives. Above all, a plan encourages all players within an organization to move in the *same direction*. And, although some players at various levels within the organization may wish to move in a different direction, a well-executed plan will describe expectations for all staff, clarifying any possible misinterpretations.

Even organizations with limited human and financial resources can undertake an effective planning process. This chapter will describe what components are necessary for the development of a sound plan: who should be involved, how to assemble the right information, as well as how to critically review key information. Development of a sound strategic plan will put your organization on the road to success with donors, clients and other key organizational constituents.

The Importance of Realistic Planning

Perhaps the most difficult situation for a director of development stems from a board that engages in unrealistic planning.

Proper planning requires realistic expectations in terms of dollar goals and time lines. Consider the organization in the following case example. Staff would have been fully capable of raising their revenue goals within a longer time frame, or with additional staffing.

When organizations seek to develop new revenues from new constituencies or to use new techniques, successful outcomes are probabilities, at best. Success depends upon adequate research, timing, staffing and allocation of resources to the new development venture. Frequently, an executive director or board develops a strategy that seeks to significantly increase results from a particular development effort. Yet, they fail to allocate sufficient resources to the task.

Such an error can negatively affect an organization and its staff. First, the staff involved in the effort may feel demoralized when they fail to reach their goal. Secondly, if the organization fails to reach the goal, an incorrect assumption may be made regarding the effectiveness of the staff or the capability of the organization itself.

Although long-term planning is essential to any program, one of the fund raising areas that seems to frequently lack proper planning is the direct mail solicitation program. Often organizations will spend thousands of dollars in launching a direct mail program, only to be disappointed by initial results. Most

---

Case Example

One very successful youth counseling center lost three directors of development within a three-year period, due to unrealistic expectations. These managers were actually setting realistic revenue goals, but they were being overshadowed by a board and development committee that not only refused to actively participate, but who also refused to follow the recommendations of the development manager. Because the organization had had an extremely successful year, doubling its revenues, the finance committee upheld that revenues could once again be doubled the following year, without any increases in staff or resources to the development function.

In the long run, the setting of unrealistic expectations proved to be extremely costly to the organization. The finance committee set an unusually high revenue goal. This not only resulted in high staff turnover, but the organization was unable to perform on a financial commitment that involved the repayment of a large balloon payment. Thus, the organization was forced to seek deficit financing, with massive layoffs of staff. Because of the management's apparent inability to manage resources, its relationship with key funders became tenuous at a time when support was urgently needed.

direct mail programs to new prospects fall short of breaking even, and may cost as much as $15 to acquire each new donor. The actual payoff of such a program does not begin to show until subsequent years, often three to five years in the future, when donors begin to renew and increase their gifts. What often happens is that a nervous, untrained, or risk-aversive board will short-circuit such development efforts before benefits actually begin to accrue.

Planning takes time and critical review from the key stakeholders of your organization

Some executive directors may see the individual solicitation campaign as a clerical function. Thus, once the solicitation letter is written, they will allow an untrained individual to manage the campaign. Although it is true that many aspects of the individual solicitation program can be managed by clerical staff, there are other aspects of the program that require technical expertise. Nonprofit organizations would achieve better results if they planned to bring in an individual with some direct mail expertise at some point in planning for the campaign.

The Strategic Plan

Time and Information: Two Key Elements in Developing a Strategic Plan

If planning is so important, why do so many managers resist it? Perhaps because effective planning takes time

and critical review from the key stakeholders of your organization. It's usually not possible to assemble a plan quickly. Often an organization may wish to shortcut the process by involving only one or two individuals. However, usually this will seriously compromise the quality and success of the plan. Without involvement from key stakeholders, it will be difficult to assess and forecast strategic direction and achieve the support necessary for full implementation.

Having the right information resources available to your planning group will also facilitate the process. Each planning participant may wish to gather materials and make them available to others in the team. Although every organization is different, some possible information resources include:

- Evaluation of competitors (see competitor analysis below);

- The SWOT analysis (see Illustration 6, following);

- Mission statement;

- Description of populations served, and any other populations that could be served in the future;

- Financial information: contributions, contracts, fees, and expenses for activities and programs;

- Internal or external survey results that affect organizational operations;

- Description or analysis of new operations or techniques that could improve the organization;

- Description of needs for human resources, programs, or facilities;

- Description of your services and their fit into the overall service delivery system within the community served.

What to Expect from a Strategic Planning Process

Strategic planning is an excellent opportunity for you and other key stakeholders to get a complete picture of your organization's goals and objectives. More specifically, planning:

- Involves volunteers, key staff, board, clients, opinion leaders, funders, and donors;

- Involves comparative research into why and how things are performing;

- Involves making decisions -- setting priorities for action;

- Involves evaluating how success will be measured, through goal setting and realistic timelines;

- Allows for strategic course adjustments, depending upon results.

The plan will be compromised if any of the above steps are short cut. Serious problems can result when organizations pursue goals that are unrelated to their key strengths, pursue projects without adequate resource support, or set unrealistic expectations.

Ideally, the strategic plan should span a minimum of three to five years. It should also include separate measurable goals for each of the organization's programs or service delivery areas. For example, the strategic plan should include separate plans for organizational development, finance, marketing, fund raising, human resources, and programs. Such detailed planning will prepare your organization for success in all aspects of its operations. It will also help the development office strengthen its proposals, public relations, individual donors appeals, and membership campaigns.

Often organizations may use an outside consultant to aid their planning efforts. If the budget allows, this is a viable method. However, with commitment of staff and time, organizations can complete their own planning process. Or, perhaps you can trade staff with another organization that wishes to complete a strategic plan. Above all, the planning process should be directed by an individual who is skillful at facilitating group processes and the organization of ideas.

Case Statement

The case statement, or case for support -- your most important marketing, fund raising, and public relations document -- is actually much more than a statement. Why is it so important to compile such a comprehensive document? A veritable resource library, excerpts from this document can be used for volunteer, staff and board training, individual and major gift solicitation, special events, and public relations. If the case has been adequately prepared, the fund raising professional and/or volunteer has only to extract the appropriate written materials appropriate for the task at hand.

Managers develop case statements for individual giving, corporate, government and foundation support, and capital support, depending on your needs. The case statement should encompass all of the following:

■ Reasons why the programs or services of the organization are important (needs statement.) Who needs the organization and why? This section should include documented need, including data, reports, or expert opinion.

■ Explanation of the organization's competitive advantage. Where does the organization fit into the general service delivery system? Why is it unique?

■ Outline of costs associated with needs and/or programs.

■ Benefits to be gained by donors or funders.

■ A thorough explanation of measurable goals and objectives: For example, will you teach 100 children to read?

■ Statements of capability. Why is the organization and its staff well suited to accomplish the stated goals? This section often includes listing of staff qualifications, awards, press releases and/or media coverage and other accomplishments.

■ Financial, organizational and legal documentation. Include copies of 990 forms, IRS determination letter, list of board of directors, audited financial statements, pie charts showing results, expenses and revenues, and donor lists.

The case should be written with a business orientation, including an emotional appeal where appropriate. In short, it must appeal to a wide variety of audiences and most importantly, the potential contributor. Therefore, as you review your case statement, you should ask yourself, Would you support the organization? Do you believe that the organization can do what it says it will do? This is best proven by testimonials from experts or users of the programs or services. Is there truly a need for what the organization is proposing? Is it supported by hard evidence, or is it more of an organizational need?

The Mission Statement

The mission statement is the foundation of your plan. It should describe, in simple language, who you serve, as well as organizational services. If you are unhappy with your current mission statement, or if it does not currently or adequately reflect your organization's work, then you may wish to redevelop the mission as your first planning step.

Some organizations have a mission that is so broad or vague that it fails to provide direction for the organization. This can seriously hamper planning efforts. On the other hand, it is entirely common for organizations to redevelop their mission as a result of insights acquired during strategic planning.

The SWOT Analysis

Planning helps an organization to determine how to allocate resources. It addresses strengths and weaknesses, opportunities and threats, as well as key internal and external factors. A key planning document is the SWOT analysis, which is shown in Illustration 6.

SWOT is the acronym for **S**trengths, **W**eaknesses, **O**pportunities and **T**hreats. Completion of this exercise will help the organization determine its future direction. When completing this exercise, it is helpful to rely upon key opinion leaders to help you chart trends and needs. Key opinion leaders may include foundation staff, government funding staff, national association staff, community leaders, competitors, donors, volunteers, and program recipients.

The case statement is the singly most important document that members of the organization will use in development.

The SWOT analysis should :

■ Identify *strengths* of programs that should continue to be developed as a primary focus, or redeveloped to serve new populations or geographic areas.

■ Identify *weaknesses* among staff, volunteers, programs, resources, and systems that should be addressed in the planning effort.

This may include the need to update office systems, the need for additional office space, or new equipment.

Staff development needs should be addressed in the plan, including budgeting for staff development. If additional staff need to be hired, this should also be included.

Other human resource needs, such as benefits and costs should be evaluated as part of the plan. An organization that provides adequate benefits is more likely to retain valuable staff. At the same time, consideration should be given to developing personnel benefit programs that are cost-effective.

■ Identify external (or outside) *opportunities* with which the organization may wish to take advantage. This may include the merger with another nonprofit organization or new populations or areas that can be served. Additionally, it may include new capabilities or services to be developed.

■ Identify *threats*, which may include current or expected competitors, as well as current directions or initiatives of the funding community.

This portion of the SWOT analysis should address the status of the organization's programs and fit into the service delivery system. Is there likely to be competition among several organizations? If so, then the organization must use the planning process to identify key strengths so that specific markets can be identified. As well, the organization may wish to eliminate or scale-back programs for which there is a declining market or need.

This is an area where quantitative information is essential. Planning participants will use data information sources to forecast numbers of clients or program participants for each planning year. Census data, survey data, and other pertinent information should be analyzed to facilitate more reliable forecasting.

Illustration 6: SWOT Analysis

SWOT ANALYSIS

Prepared for Vetserve: a nonprofit organization serving veterans.

Strengths
- Vetserve's employment programs for veterans meet an urgent and continuing need.
- Vetserve has strong capabilities in serving veterans.
- Many veteran volunteers already support Vetserve (100) and more are available in the surrounding urban area.

Weaknesses (internal)
- Database programs and internal computer systems are seriously outdated.
- Vetserve's program for young adults has been experiencing poor enrollment since it was started in 1994.
- Vetserve has poor public visibility outside the immediate Twin City area.
- Staff and budget support for fund raising and public relations is minimal.
- Fund raising staff need training in marketing and public relations.
- Few marketing communications have been developed.
- The employment program offices need updating and expansion of an additional 5,000 square feet.

Opportunities
- An anticipated 5% of the total number of veterans (250,000- 300,000) need services that are being provided by other agencies or organizations.
- St. Cloud has a hospital that could be a collaborator or a competitor.
- Veterans are heavy sweepstakes users. VFW clubs locally may be candidates for joint sweepstakes promotions to veterans.
- Needs for wholistic health are not being met by other service providers. Each tends to serve only a particular aspect of health or benefits, making it necessary for a veteran to be a member or participant of all programs. This tends to isolate veterans, and many are unaware of opportunities. Vetserve could provide information about what is available and encourage access.
- The local federal office is expected to cut back employment programs for veterans in 1997. Depending upon the extent of the cutbacks, this might increase the need for Vetserve programs.

Threats (external)
- Collaboration may be difficult to obtain among the many varied veteran serving organizations.
- Two other veteran serving organizations (VVA and DVV) have strong fund raising capabilities, encouraging a strongly competitive environment.
- Positive public sentiment towards veterans is minimal during peacetime.
- Federal funding for veteran programs is being scaled back. This leaves a large portion of Vetserve's budget (20%) at-risk.
- The owner of the bulding that houses the nutrition program has been talking about selling the building. Vetserve may need to develop or find an alternative site.

Research: the Key Competitor Analysis

If the competitor analysis is completed with a high level of detail, staff will note geographic areas of dominance, degree of service to specific populations, and other important data.

Accurate positioning of your organization in relation to others in the field will help your organization to retain a favorable market position amidst an intensely competive environment.

One tool to help you is the competitor analysis, shown in Illustration 7. Diligent attention to the work of your competitors will assist you in developing a plan that meets community needs. You may wish to avoid developing programs where there is significant competition or which are operated by competitors with significant expertise. On the other hand, if your organization's philosophy is different, but nonetheless effective, then the burden of proof will be upon your organization to demonstrate its capability.

Foundations are often interested in knowing how an organization fits into the service delivery system. Thus, if a proposal lacks the ability to portray that an organization's services are needed or unduplicated, then it will often fail to receive the necessary funding. Similarly, an appeal to individual donors must discriminate the organization as a leader among a field of *perceived* competitors. Your primary goal must be to dispel these unfounded beliefs and/or opinions that stand in the way of donated support.

The key competitor analysis is a matrix that describes the organization's key competitors. Occasionally, staff may have difficulty identifying competitors. Nonetheless, you should be able to identify what organizational services or programs are unique. Staff may discover that there are different competitors for different programs within the organization. In this case, it may be useful to develop a separate key competitor analysis for each of the distinct service areas within the organization.

One of the best ways to complete your research is to consult your local United Way directory and nonprofit directories. This is an exercise that will benefit any program planner. Often, competitors will surface that are virtually unknown. Foundation directories and annual reports of major corporations and/or foundations also will supply you with a list of organizations that they have supported. A corporation funding another organization similar to yours is likely to be sympathetic to your cause, but you will still need to prove that your organization is providing additional needed services.

If the key competitor analysis is completed with a high level of detail, staff will be able to note geographic areas of dominance, degree of service to specific populations, and other important data. Once this matrix is completed, a Service Configuration Matrix can be completed to give a more comprehensive picture.

Still, a comprehensive competitor analysis usually requires more than just compiling information. You may need to visit or meet with your competitors in order to ask specific questions about their programs. This is often the first step toward developing excellence in program design. When channels of communication are opened between competing organizations, it often results in better programming to suit the needs of the target populations. Organizations may wish to form strategic alliances, or follow certain strategic directions based on their own unique organizational capabilities.

Service Configuration Matrix

The Service Configuration Matrix provides a bird's eye-view of the scope of an organization's services, including (1) target populations and (2) percentage of share in service delivery. From this perspective, planners can begin to answer the following questions:

- Is the organization an expert or dominant player in a particular arena?

- Are there others with greater capability in certain areas?

- Would it be a wise decision to drop programs with only marginal services to a minimal number of

individuals? Or do these programs serve other functions for the organization?

Are there pockets of individuals who are going unserved? For example, in the Service Configuration Matrix in the following illustration, VETSERVE serves many diverse populations, but they must qualify under public assistance. This may indicate that there are others who may also need services-those who do not qualify for public assistance.

Completion of the Service Configuration Matrix demonstrates how the organization fits into the service delivery system, illustrating duplication of services and underserved populations. Thus, the organizational planners and development staff can begin to shape strategic plans as well as develop positioning strategies for the organization.

Constituency Circle

Development managers use the Constituency Circle to identify constituents and potential strategies for their cultivation. When the numbers are inserted, with specifics about the type of constituent, it assists the manager in viewing the entire spectrum of organizational stakeholders. In this manner, the manager can begin to formulate comparisons between constituencies, prioritize constituencies, and develop targeted strategies.

Illustration 7: Key Competitor Analysis for a Direct Mail Fund Raising Program
Level of current direct mail fund raising activity - little * ------ **** more

	Organization	Target Population	Programs	Geography	Other
**	VETSERVE VS	Developmental Disabilities Adults Traumatic Brain Injury Mental Retardation Seniors (w/wo disability)	Residential Program Vocational Program Community Integration (TBI) Assembly/Packaging Workshop Job Placement	Minnesota	320 business partners Budget: $9 million Endowment 350 individual/business donors
**	Veterans Varied Associations VVA	Women Chemical Dependents Adults Corrections Chemical Dependents Severe physical/sensory disabilities Severe mentally ill	6 Programs in vocational training/placement Employment Advocacy: (dislocated worker, veterans, low income) Aid to independent living	Hennepin/Sherburne counties 7 county area predominates	300 individual/business donors Budget: $9 million
****	Veterans Center	Adults Children Sensory impairments Children	Physical Rehabilitation Vocational Program Medical model Vocational training, placement Collaborate w/ Robbinsdale Schools (GED) Resident and Day Camps Assisted living/transitional housing Medical/mental health/other therapies Recreational/social activities	Minnesota State: Significant activity	Budget: $16 million
***	Disabled Veterans of the Valley	Adults / children Vocational disabilities	Vocational training, workshops, employment on-site/community	Ramsey/Anoka/Hennepin counties	Budget: $5 million

Illustration 8: Service Configuration Matrix
Three primary organizations within service delivery system: VS, DVV, and VVA. Market share in four service categories.

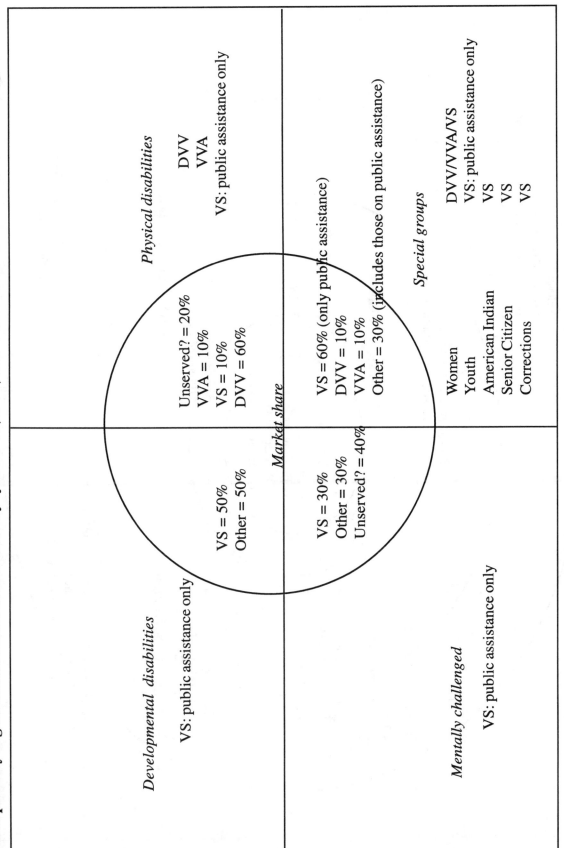

Physical disabilities

DVV
VVA

VS: public assistance only

Unserved? = 20%
VVA = 10%
VS = 10%
DVV = 60%

Special groups

DVV/VVA/VS
VS: public assistance only
VS
VS
VS

Women
Youth
American Indian
Senior Citizen
Corrections

VS = 60% (only public assistance)
DVV = 10%
VVA = 10%
Other = 30% (includes those on public assistance)

Market share

Developmental disabilities

VS: public assistance only

VS = 50%
Other = 50%

VS = 30%
Other = 30%
Unserved? = 40%

Mentally challenged

VS: public assistance only

Illustration 9:

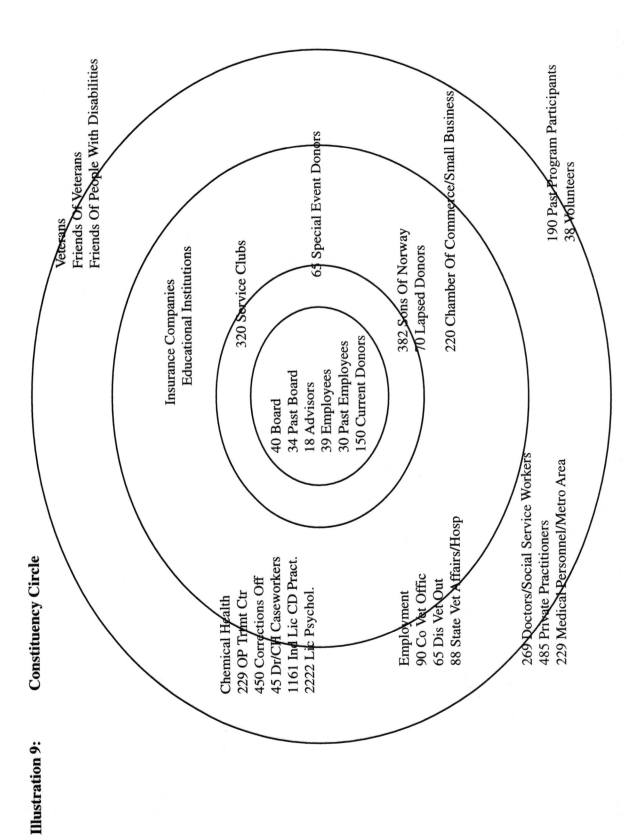

Constituency Circle

Veterans
Friends Of Veterans
Friends Of People With Disabilities

Insurance Companies
Educational Institutions

320 Service Clubs

65 Special Event Donors

40 Board
34 Past Board
18 Advisors
39 Employees
30 Past Employees
150 Current Donors

382 Sons Of Norway
70 Lapsed Donors

220 Chamber Of Commerce/Small Business

190 Past Program Participants
38 Volunteers

Chemical Health
229 OP Trtmt Ctr
450 Corrections Off
45 Dr/CH Caseworkers
1161 Ind Lic CD Pract.
2222 Lic Psychol.

Employment
90 Co Vet Offic
65 Dis Vet Out
88 State Vet Affairs/Hosp

269 Doctors/Social Service Workers
485 Private Practitioners
229 Medical Personnel/Metro Area

Constituency Circle:

Most likely candidates for giving are located in innermost circles

For example, a fund raising committee may wish to view the Constituency Circle to prioritize who to solicit, how they will be solicited, and who will manage such a solicitation. In the Constituency Circle in Illustration 9, it becomes more clear that the 2,222 licensed psychologists might be prospects for a personalized letter from an organizational volunteer who holds a position of leadership within the Psychologists Association. Similarly, a different type of event would be developed for 65 special event donors than if the organization had 4,000 special event donors.

Evaluation

What kinds of results has your organization achieved? Can they be improved? If you can answer these two questions, then you will have established the foundation of an effective development office.

Answering these questions requires setting up the proper measurement systems. It means evaluating the various components of fund raising, marketing, and public relations at various critical times throughout the year. It may also mean investing in computer or administrative systems and using various methods of inquiry. Setting up measurement systems will actually save you money in the long run, because they will help you spend your limited dollars most effectively.

The following are examples of helpful evaluation systems:

- What are the comparative results for different fund raising methods for different years? Looking at a long-term (3-5 years) scheme of methods will help you identify what is working and what is not.

- Segmenting the database: what are the revenues from each donor or membership segment? You may discover that certain segments of your database respond more favorably to different types of appeals. Similarly, by looking at different segments of your program participants, you may discover which groups are responding more favorably to appeals and which segments should receive reduced activity.

An effective relational database program allows you to evaluate groups within groups. Thus, you may be able to compare females versus males, seniors versus youth participants, or make any other comparison for which you have fields within your database. For example, you may discover that a special appeal for a resource library receives higher donation amounts from participants in your language services program than from your parenting program.

Of course, this doesn't necessarily

mean that you will stop soliciting participants from your parenting program. Rather, it means that you may consider spending more of your limited resources in the areas that are the most productive. It is usually more cost effective to cultivate results from a group that is performing well rather than to try to improve results from a group that exhibits lackluster performance. Here again, you, the development manager, must decide on the best options for your limited resources.

■ What are the reactions of your key publics to your programs? Savvy organizations send regular surveys or implement focus groups and questionnaires to compile this information. These can be extremely expensive and sophisticated, or simple and low cost. Survey design depends upon the type of information needed as well as numerous other criteria such as the budget available, the appropriateness to the target audience, time, as well as the expertise available.

Care should be taken when developing evaluation instruments. Some staff, after developing sophisticated questionnaires, discover that they have little need for all the information gathered. Before including a question in the survey, ask yourself how you will use this information. Naturally, volumes of information are not useful if there is not sufficient time to review and compile the information for future evaluation. Finally, care should be given that the questions are understandable by the target audience, and that they are free from biases that can influence the answers of the respondents.

Even though *quick and dirty* surveys usually provide only minimal information, they can also provide important data. Here are a few ideas for implementing the low-cost variety:

■ Ask a simple question on the reply device (the mail back pledge card) of your direct-mail package. One organization simply asked donors if they would allow their name to be rented or sold. The package that asked this question had better results than the package that didn't.

■ Send out a survey in your newsletter. Make the questions easy to answer and include a return envelope.

■ Ask a pertinent question or two on your next phone solicitation campaign.

You will probably discover that most donors or individuals like to be asked for their opinion, as long as it doesn't take an extraordinary amount of time. If you structure your questions correctly, you will discover that you'll receive extremely valuable information that will ultimately help you to make better decisions.

As you progress, you will discover how to improve your questionnaires to eliminate confusion. One excellent book that discusses how to develop surveys is *The Survey Research Handbook*, by Pamela L. Alreck and Robert B. Settle. (Irwin, Homewood, Illinois, 1985). One way to improve your questionnaires is to field-test them with a small group of individuals before they are finalized. Often this will identify any confusing examples.

Naturally, it is wise to plan for someone to complete the data tabulation on your surveys. If you don't have the time to do this, or cannot identify volunteers or interns to assist you, then you shouldn't waste your time developing the survey.

Review Checklist

√ Does your organization have a current strategic plan that charts organizational efforts?

√ Have all key stakeholders, volunteers, clients, donors, board members, and key advisors been involved in the development of the plan?

√ Does your organization have a mission statement that adequately reflects who the organization serves and the services it provides? Does it adequately differentiate the organization from its competitors? Is it simple to understand?

√ As part of its planning process, has your organization surveyed the outside environment, as well as the internal environment to ascertain strengths, weaknesses, opportunities, and threats? (SWOT analysis)

√ Does your organization's program and development staff understand how the organization fits into the overall service delivery system? Is there thorough knowledge of competitors, if any, as well as gaps, and a continuum of services or products to meet existing needs (competitor analysis)?

√ Does your organization have an ongoing plan for evaluation of its programs, services, products, and promotions?

Conclusion

Taking the time to plan will pay off immeasurably. Planning forces you to evaluate and select the best alternatives for your investment of time and finances. Further, planning enables you to set time management schedules so you can anticipate peak work periods, thereby allowing you time to recruit or train volunteers and/or contractual or paid staff.

If you are already planning your work, you are to be congratulated. Consider how your plan fits with others within the organization or as part of the overall organizational plan. When all key players are planning and working towards similar goals, the outcomes begin to multiply!

PUBLIC RELATIONS & MARKETING

- ■ *How to Identify Your Key Publics*

- ■ *Public Relations and the Donor*

- ■ *Public Relations and the Board: Nine Easy Ideas*

- ■ *Public Relations and the Employee*

- ■ *Public Relations and External Publics*

- ■ *Simple Steps to Effective Media Relations*

- ■ *Donor/Membership Segmentation Strategies*

- ■ *Free and Low-Cost Marketing Ideas*

- ■ *Key Questions for Successful Events*

CHAPTER

5

INTRODUCTION

Public relations is as integral a part of your fund raising plan as the donor return envelope. Yet, how many nonprofit organizations actively engage in public relations? A strong public relations program is more than television or newspaper coverage or adequate enrollment for your special events. Effective public relations includes planning and implementation of specific activities and marketing communications for all of the individuals who may take an interest in your organization, also known as your key publics.

Development professionals face many challenges in trying to manage relationships with key publics. The cost of marketing communications has increased significantly, and the proliferation of competing messages in the marketplace provides a confusing backdrop for any media campaign. Moreover, an increasingly diverse population requires strategies that respond to diverse needs and cultures, in content, style, and/or tone. Managers need to develop a variety of cost-effective marketing communications to reach these varied audiences.

The most important step to improve the effectiveness of your public relations and save valuable time and dollars is to identify and prioritize your organization's key publics. This chapter will provide you with tools to help you accomplish this task.

Your organization's key publics are both external (outside of the organization) and internal (employees, board members, donors, members, and volunteers.) Further, each public requires a distinctively different communications strategy, with specific messages and strategies tied to their unique interests. Launching a campaign that uses the same method to reach all of an organization's key publics is simply not advisable.

An organization may have many key publics, both external and internal, each of which require a distinctively different communications strategy.

This chapter will discuss how to cultivate these key relationships in cost-effective ways, through print, technology, and broadcast media. We'll present options for you to consider in segmenting your organization's publics. These segmentation strategies will help you to develop specific marketing communications for different publics, making them more *relevant, cost-effective, and message-appropriate.*

Lastly, this chapter will present a sampling of many low-cost or no-cost ideas in marketing communications as well as a checklist for planning your next special event.

Customer Communications Take Center Stage

Continual, in-depth communication with key stakeholders is an essential element for any organization. This means listening to customer needs, designing programs to meet these needs and maintaining continual program improvement related to customer needs. The following story of Child's Play Theatre Company exemplifies the growth that occurs when an organization incorporates this communication strategy at the heart of everything it does — from board involvement to program development.

Case Example

In 1984, the environment for theater arts in the Minneapolis-St. Paul area was in a turbulent state. One of the area's major theaters was in crisis. It had not yet clearly solidified what type of programs it would develop and its exact audiences were unknown. From this amorphous environment sprung the Child's Play Theatre Company, piloted by a group of parents and artists who felt that education should be married to the theater arts for young people. This founding group believed that they would find a welcome audience amidst the growing population in the western suburbs of the Minneapolis area.

Their hunches proved correct. By 1988, the theater had begun to serve 25,000 people yearly, with a budget of $110,000. At that time they were profitable enough to hire a new executive director to begin to manage many of the affairs that had formerly been managed by volunteers and board members. The new executive director explained to the board that if the company wished to grow, that it must develop a more professional management approach. Board members must no longer manage the operational affairs of the organization. Instead, they would shift their focus to governing organizational policies and operations while staff managed the day-to-day activities. To make this change happen as smoothly as possible, additional staff would be hired.

This was a change not welcomed by all. Some board members resisted relinquishing the culture of the *hands-on* board. What was clear to the new executive was that there needed to be a clear separation of power between board and staff, with responsibilities clearly defined. It would take three years of hard work before this goal would be accomplished.

In the fall of 1988, the board approved the hiring of a marketing and outreach manager. The theater would need to depend almost solely on earned revenues, since fund raising was minimal, and amounted to only nine percent or $10,000 of the organizational budget. The marketing director was hired for her abilities to expand programming. She sent written surveys to hundreds of contacts, including school teachers, parents, community leaders and other key constituents. One particular question was designed to measure the likelihood that audiences would accept a residency program: "How likely is your organization to book a residency company?" If the respondent answered positively, the next question asked what the probable sources of project funds would be. In this manner, the organization was able to determine the likelihood of the program succeeding as well as probable funding sources, two key questions that should be answered before launching any new venture.

The marketing director continued to maintain ongoing contact with key customers: the parents and teachers of elementary-age children. Communications focused on obtaining answers as to what type of programming the children liked and what teachers and parents viewed as important. Customers frequently requested educational experiences in theater that explored violence prevention, peer-to-peer harassment, HIV/AIDS awareness and self-esteem. Armed with this powerful knowledge, the Child's Play Theatre Company was able to develop specific programming that was ideally suited to the needs, interests, and financial resources of its key stakeholders.

By 1990, two years later, the theater had earned a respected position within the community. Prior to this, the theater had had lackluster performance in fund raising, receiving grants only through board contacts. By this time, however, three major corporate funders were willing to support the theater's work. The annual budget was now $308,000. Nineteen percent of the total was being contributed by individual and corporate donors (including a small state grant of $5,000.)

Today, the Child's Play Theatre Company has begun to think about expanding its audiences beyond its primary area of expertise, from elementary-age children to middle-school and high-school audiences. Recognizing that its audiences have unique needs, the theater has sought to address its programming appropriately. Helping a local high school to produce its own play, while assuming 75 percent of the financial risk of the investment, is proving to be a worthwhile tactic. In this way, the older audiences retain the opportunity to design and produce the play, while benefiting from the technical assistance provided by Child's Play Theatre Company.

By 1996, the theater's annual budget had grown to more than half a million dollars (more than four times what it had been seven years earlier). Approximately $125,000 of the total budget is now raised from contributions. Maintaining their responsiveness to community needs, staff continue to maintain ongoing dialog with key stakeholders.

The annual survey is foremost among the organization's planning tools. It regularly provides valuable information from the organization's key publics, identifying their needs, opinions, and preferences. This information gives direction to organizational planning and marketing efforts. The most recently completed surveys for individuals and groups appear on the following pages.

Illustration 10-1: Child's Play Theater Individual Member Survey, page 1

Individual

Child's Play Theatre Company
Audience Member Survey

Dear Patron:

    Thank you for attending Child's Play Theatre Company. Your patronage is very important to us and we look forward to serving you again during our 1996-97 season. In an effort to more effectively serve our valued patrons we are conducting a survey requesting feedback about our programming and services. We ask that you assist us by completing the following survey, and returning it to us by April 15. We will use the results of this survey as a tool to guide us in providing our customers with improved services and communications. Thank you for your time.

1)   What do you like most about CPTC? Please <u>rank</u> the following choices in order of preference.
    1 = like the most...6 = like the least
    _____Quality of productions   _____Theatre facilities
    _____Youth cast   _____Play selection
    _____Price   _____Location of Theatre
    _____Performance times

    Please comment on any of the above:_____
    _____

2)   How did you <u>originally</u> hear about CPTC? (Check all that apply)
    _____newspaper ad, which publication?_____
    _____word of mouth
    _____school flyer
    _____television, which station?_____
    _____radio, which station?_____
    _____newspaper calendar listing, which publication?_____
    _____other_____

3)   Which of the following publications do you read regularly? (Check all that apply)
    _____Minnesota Parent   _____Minnesota Monthly
    _____Family Times   _____City Pages
    _____Star Tribune   _____Twin City Reader
    _____Pioneer Press   _____Sun Publications
    _____Skyway/Freeway News   _____Other,_____
    _____Mpls St Paul magazine

4)   How do you usually find out about CPTC programming? Could be more than one answer.
    _____

5)   What are the ages of the children with whom you attend CPTC performances? (Check all that apply)
    _____I do not bring any children   _____8-11 years
    _____0-3 years   _____12-15 years
    _____4-7 years   _____16 + years

6)   Please comment on the quality and content of our on-going communication materials.
    Newsletter_____
    Production playbill_____
    School flyers_____

7)   Is there another method by which you would like us to communicate to you?_____

8)   Is there a play or story that you would like to see us produce?_____

-OVER PLEASE-

Illustration 10-2: Child's Play Theatre Company Individual Member Survey, page 2

9) Is there a service you would like to see us provide, or is there something you feel we could improve upon?_____
_____

10) Do you plan to attend our theater again? Circle one: Yes No
If no, why not?_____

The following questions are optional:

11) What is your age?
_____20-30 years   _____41-50 years
_____31-40 years   _____51 or more years

12) What is your marital status?
_____Single (never married)
_____Divorced
_____Married
_____Widowed

13) Do you own or rent? (Please circle one)

14) What is the last education level you completed (Check one)
_____High school
_____Some college
_____Technical school
_____4 years college or more

15) Please describe your occupation _____

16) What is the range of your combined household income?
_____under $15,000   _____$45,001-$55,000
_____$15,001-$25,000   _____$55,001-$65,000
_____$25,001-$35,000   _____$65,001-$75,000
_____$35,001-$45,000   _____Greater than $75,000

Thank you for taking the time to complete this survey.
Your feedback is important to us.

Please mail your completed survey to us or drop it off at the box office
next time you attend a performance at our theatre.

Our mailing address is:
Child's Play Theatre Company
1719 Mainstreet
Hopkins, MN 55343

Attention: Jill Booher

Illustration 11-1: Child's Play Theatre Company Group Member Survey, page 1

Group

Child's Play Theatre Company
Audience Member Survey

Dear Group Leader:

    Thank you for attending Child's Play Theatre Company. Your patronage is very important to us and we look forward to serving you again during our 1996-97 season. In an effort to more effectively serve our valued patrons we are conducting a survey requesting feedback about our programming and services. We ask that you assist us by completing the following survey, and returning it to us by May 15. We will use the results of this survey as a tool to guide us in providing our customers with improved services and communications. Thank you for your time.

1)   What do you like most about CPTC? Please <u>rate</u> the following choices in order of preference.
    1 = like the most...6 = like the least
    _____Quality of productions   _____Theatre facilities
    _____Youth cast   _____Play selection
    _____Price   _____Location of Theatre
    _____Performance times

    Please comment on any of the above:_____
    _____

2)   How did you <u>originally</u> hear about CPTC? (Check all that apply)
    _____Newspaper ad, which publication?_____
    _____School flyer
    _____Television, which station?_____
    _____Radio, which station?_____
    _____Brochure
    _____Newspaper calendar listing, which publication?_____
    _____Associate_____
    _____Other_____

3)   Which of the following publications do you read regularly? (check all that apply)
    ____Minnesota Parent   ____Minnesota Monthly
    ____Family Times   ____City Pages
    ____StarTribune   ____Twin City Reader
    ____Pioneer Press   ____Sun Publications
    ____Skyway/Freeway News   ____Other
    ____Mpls St Paul magazine

4)   How do you usually hear about CPTC programming? Could be more than one answer.
    _____

5)   Is there a service that you would like to see us provide, or is there something that you feel we could improve upon?_____
    _____

6)   Are you aware that CPTC provides quality school outreach programs? Please circle one: Yes No
    If yes, how did you hear about our outreach programs?_____

7)   In what grades are the children with whom you have attended CPTC performances? (Check all that apply)
    _____Pre - First   _____4th - 5th
    _____2nd - 3rd   _____5th and up
    _____Other

-OVER PLEASE-

Illustration 11-2: Child's Play Theatre Company Group Member Survey, page 2

8) In addition to attending Child's Play Theatre Company during the year, do you also attend other area youth theaters. Yes No
If yes, please indicate which theater(s)_____

9) What is our most effective method of communication to you?
Please Rate: 1 = most effective... 5 = least effective.
_____Playbill   _____School flyers
_____Season brochure   _____Letters
_____Other, please describe_____

10) Is there another method by which you would like us to communicate to you?_____
----

11) Do you find our Theatre Guide to be a useful educational tool?
----

12) Is there a play or story that you would like to see us produce?_____
----

13) Do you plan to attend a CPTC performance next season?
Please circle one: Yes No
If No, why not?_____

Thank you for taking the time to complete this survey.
Your feedback is important to us.

Please mail your completed survey to us or drop it off at the box office
next time you attend a performance at our theatre.

Our mailing address is:
Child's Play Theatre Company
1719 Mainstreet
Hopkins, MN 55343

Attention: Jill Booher

The Child's Play Theatre Company is an example of a nonprofit organization that stayed focused on its mission. Too often, organizations jump quickly to new ventures, new locations, and new audiences. Still, the organization that looks introspectively at its own strengths and weaknesses, as measured against community need, will find fertile ground for growth. Growth can also be found in the more subtle changes that improve programming. The story of Child's Play Theatre Company illustrates the results that can be obtained from (1) recognizing organizational strengths, (2) seizing opportunities as they occur, and (3) designing programs with a continual eye towards community needs.

The Public Relations Plan

The first step in any publicity campaign is to determine your specific objectives. Do you want your target population to call in and enroll for a class? Do you want them to make a donation? Do you want them to attend a charity ball or participate in a special benefit event? Knowing the desired outcome will help you identify who may be most interested and help you develop the corresponding strategy to reach them.

The individuals who are most likely to be influenced by your messages are known as your *key publics*. Every organization has several different publics who are the *stakeholders* of the organization. For example, for a youth-serving organization, the *key publics, or stakeholders* of the organization may be board members, committee members, parents, teachers, foundations who fund youth programs, law enforcement personnel, and the youth served.

No organization or company ever has enough resources to develop a campaign to reach all of its publics. Therefore, it is necessary to segment and rank your publics so that you can best determine where to spend your limited resources. Once you know who your key publics are, you will be better prepared to do more research on their interests and needs, or in some cases, to go ahead and design the communications strategy to reach them.

To help you complete this task, a Key Public Matrix is shown in Illustration 12.

Explanation for Key Public Matrix

Observe the first row of horizontal boxes. They illustrate key publics for a youth-serving organization. Many organizations will have several different publics to consider. As you begin to identify your publics, you may run out of space. Thus, two or three copies of this chart may be necessary.

Similarly, different sets of charts could be filled out for each marketing or fund raising campaign. If used in this manner, you will begin to see how communications can be integrated, or used together, to multiply the effects from different marketing media.

For example, if you consider that two of your key publics may have the same interests or needs, then a single communication piece might be designed to reach these publics. You may find that it takes a considerable amount of time to thoroughly identify and evaluate all of the categories on the chart. Additionally, you may need to do some research at the public library to gain more information about these key publics.

Once you have completed the matrix, however, you will be well prepared to develop the strategy and tactics to communicate key ideas and move your publics to action. Depending upon the level of detail, the matrix also functions as a blueprint for other staff, volunteers and board members to conceptualize the marketing communications plan for a campaign. Moreover, the chart will be your historic document and partner in developing all of your marketing and fund raising activities for many months into the future.

Illustration 12: Key Public Matrix　　　**Project: Special Event Dinner**　　　**Organization: Youth Today**

Priority Rank	Public	Benefits to/ Interests of Public	Quantity/ Communication	Competitive Selling Strategies
1	Board Members	Social opportunity/ entertainment Fulfills responsibility to meet financial needs of organization	10 invitees/ hand addressed invitations	Notable celebrities, music, food
2	Board Member personal contacts	Social opportunity/ entertainment Respect for personal relationship to board members	100 invitees/ hand addressed invitations (each board member sends to 10 contacts)	Notable celebrities, music, food
3	Youth and family program volunteers	Social opportunity/ entertainment Supports a community need	40 invitees/ hand addressed invitations	Notable celebrities, music, food
4	Current and Past Donors and Members	Social opportunity/ entertainment Supports a community need	5,000 invitees/ brochure sent in bulk direct mail package	Notable celebrities, music, food, excellent value

Note: An explanation of the key public matrix appears on the preceding page

Public Relations and the Individual Donor

Regular communications with donors
is central to membership and donor
retention. The following case example
highlights one organization's success
in developing varied communication
strategies for its donor publics.
Equally important to your membership
and individual giving programs is a
regular program for donor or member
acknowledgment and recognition. A
more detailed description of donor
acknowledgment and recognition
appears in chapter 9.

Case Example

The Emergency FoodShelf, a nonprofit network serving 23 community sites, had experienced strong growth in its programs throughout its more than twenty-year history. In 1993, however, the executive director noticed a disturbing trend: even though the organization was now bringing in nearly $300,000 from individual donors and small businesses, the total revenues had declined for the past two years. Even more distressing, the need for programs was greater than ever, increasing at all of its sites, for all age groups served.

In addition to administrative duties, the executive director was managing grants and gifts from individuals. She felt she simply didn't have the time to trouble shoot the problem of declining revenues. It was time to bring in a specialist.

That year, Hodiak Development was brought in to assess the current situation and make any changes that would reverse the decline. The first task was to assess the segments within the organization's database, evaluating the number of donors and total revenues.

The organization had not been using any segmentation strategies; the same letter was normally sent to all donors, regardless of the size of their prior gifts. Although there were 10,000 names on the house file, only 5,000 were current donors. No fund raising software was in use. The food shelf had a customized database that made reporting and segmentation more difficult. Hence, all individuals had been mailed the same communication, whether they were a current, past, or lapsed donor.

To begin, Hodiak grouped and subgrouped the names in the house file (the existing database file), using the following categories:

- CURRENT; Current donors giving within the last year;

- LYBNT; Donors who have skipped a year in giving. It has been more than 12 months, but 24 months or less since their last gift *(last year but not this year);*

- PYBNT; Past donors, have not given for more than 24 months *(past year but not this year).*

Within each of these groups, separate categories were made for donors, at the following levels:
- Less than $15
- $15 - $149
- $150 and above.

Case Example, continued

When a chart was made to show the number of gifts at various donor levels, it indicated that very few donors were giving at levels above $100. A small percentage (2%) of donors were giving multiple gifts throughout the year.

Following Hodiak's recommendations, the board chose the following strategy: (1) to survey lapsed donors to determine if and how they should be encouraged to start giving again, (2) to try to upgrade the size of donor gifts, and (3) to try to increase overall revenues. Because fund raising was becoming increasingly competitive, it was recommended that the organization begin to segment its donors, developing unique strategies and communications for each group.

Simply stated, the segmentation strategies were as follows:

- Donors giving at lower levels (less than $15) would be sent generic appeals, without a personalized salutation.

- Current donors and donors at higher levels of giving would be sent personalized letters, in a #10 closed-face (non-window) envelope. These would be mailed at the bulk rate, although a bulk enditia stamp would not be used. Instead, in order to add a personalized touch, a machine-applied pre-canceled stamp would be used. The dollar cutoff for this segment differed for each mailing but generally targeted gifts in the $50 to $100 range.

- Donors giving at $100 and above would be sent a hand-signed, personalized letter in a closed face #10 envelope.

- Lapsed donors who had not given for three years or more would be sent a survey asking them for their opinions and also asking for a gift.

The response to the personalized letter to current donors (up to $100) was tremendous. At a 24% response rate, with an average gift of $62, it netted more than the organization had ever received from this same segment. By comparison, a non-personalized letter sent to the same donor group 40 days later had a 11.74% response rate (These two packages were different and were dropped in the mail on different dates. Therefore, they cannot truly be compared with one another. Nonetheless, because of the vast difference in response rate, one can certainly make a case for personalization!) The non-personalized letter, brochure, reply device, and envelope appear in Illustrations 13-1 through 13-5.

Lapsed donors responded favorably to the survey, with 2.98% returning contributions along with the completed survey. This response rate is typical for donors who have not been giving to the organization for several years. The response rate from lapsed donors is often similar to "prospects," or a "cold list" that has never been mailed.

In addition to the revenue received, responses indicated that many past donors were not familiar with the need for emergency food. Many felt that they were already addressing this need by giving to their church and therefore did not feel the need to give to the community food shelf network. These responses helped the organization chart new strategies of communication for these past donors. Clearly, donors needed to be informed about the need for emergency food as well as why the food shelf needed to be supported in its work with churches, in neighborhoods, and with local organizations. Lastly, few knew about the extremely low fund raising costs of the organization.

In order to increase awareness of these needs, a quarterly newsletter was developed. Mailed to 10,000 names on the organization's house file, the newsletter would bring in nearly $10,000 in gifts each time it was mailed. (Newsletters are not typically considered high-revenue communication tools, but they seemed to work for this organization).

In addition to reversing the downward trend and substantially increasing its revenues that year (up 11%), Emergency Food Shelf Network overcame other challenges. First, it became apparent how important it was to have an effective database system for tracking. Two years later, the organization made a decision to upgrade its systems.

Secondly, board and staff realized the importance of a communications and public relations plan. A yearly plan was developed for each donor segment, including the types of communications as well as mailing dates and quantities. This plan and schedule enabled the organization to buy envelopes and other supplies in bulk, saving a significant amount in printing costs.

In sum, although there is much to be learned from this example, it is important that each organization develop its own systems for donor communications. How an organization segments its donors depends on many factors: how many donors are at each level, how frequently the organization wishes to mail, and the staff and financial

---

Case Example, continued

resources available for the task. The community food shelf network had limited staff and resources it could devote to the fund raising effort. Equally important is that it had few donors (other than corporate and foundation gifts) at levels above $150. Because of this, a number of segments were grouped together for efficiency. An organization with larger numbers of donors at various levels may wish to have more segments.

From an operational viewpoint, an organization with limited staff may wish to have much of the mail assembly work done outside the office. The community food shelf actually had the letters personalized, assembled, and delivered to the post office by an outside vendor. This proved to be their most cost-effective alternative to in-house mail preparation.

Illustration 13-1: Emergency Foodshelf Network direct mail letter, front side

**Emergency FoodShelf
Network, Inc.**
1400 - 12th Avenue Northeast
Minneapolis, MN 55413-1602
(612) 788-7777

November 23, 1993

Dear Friend:

She was absolutely pitiful....her tiny body hunched over like rag doll.

"Momma....my stomach hurts," Sara whimpered softly.

Sara's mother had heard her cries before. She knew what the problem was......but her options for helping Sara were limited.

With this week's paycheck she had had to buy shoes for Sara's rapidly growing feet. Then, after paying the bills, she had $7.15 left over to buy food for the entire week.

To make things worse...........she was ineligible for any supplementary food programs.

No wonder Sara had hunger pains.   Now, all her mother had to give her was some day-old bread.

It breaks my heart to see children like Sara.

Because, I know that...........when hunger knocks at the door, over and over again..... children face serious problems:

They are more prone to illness...

they find it difficult to learn in school...

and all else in life becomes secondary.

Studies show that as many as **1 out of every 8 children experience hunger** on a regular basis. (Food Research and Action Center)

I fear for their future.......these children are so vulnerable.
And...today...times are worse than ever for children who experience hunger......

We absolutely must help them!

Luckily, Emergency Foodshelf Network provides the help families need when times are tough.   That's why we ask you to give generously.

You'll join a caring community of individuals who support our fight against hunger......

Please turn over to other side........

Illustration 13-2: Emergency Foodshelf Network direct mail letter, page 2

Some have supported our efforts every year, as the hunger problem has grown, increasingly...............to significant levels....... right here in Minneapolis and surrounding suburbs.

This year, we must stretch our resources beyond that of 1992, in order to serve more families. Because......<u>food requests are up by 5000 more than last year.</u>

If you have already made a gift, it is deeply appreciated.....But, we still must increase our contributions:.... even more this year.

You, see, we must reach our goal of $150,000 by year-end 1993......... in order to serve all of these people.

And, we want to keep our emergency foodshelves open....in all parts of Hennepin County.

<u>Without your support, many families like Sara's won't have holiday</u> dinners. In fact.....some may not have food at all.

Your gift, however, will make the holidays infinitely better for these families.

Even more, we'll spend **as much as 95 cents of every dollar directly on our food programs.** Because....we spend substantially less in administrative and fundraising expenses than other organizations.

<u>What better investment could you make</u> this holiday season..........that would so significantly impact the lives of others?

Here's what your gift makes possible:

Donation	Meals provided
$25	35
$45	66
$100	147
$200	294

But, no matter what the size of your gift....it will help.

Please don't delay.......we need your support immediately...for our holiday food program.

Sincerely,

signature deleted at the request of the organization

P.S. Mail your tax-deductible check today.....and make this holiday a special one for the children and families who face hunger.

Illustration 13-3: Emergency Foodshelf Direct Mail Brochure (front and back)

Join the Fight Against Hunger......

Persistent hunger strikes with vengeance at the well-being of men, women and children.....rendering them vulnerable to illness and incapacity. Your gift will fight hunger by supplying nutritious meals and emergency food to many needy people.

Monetary contributions: the most efficient way to donate
Because we operate so effectively, we are able to secure food at greatly reduced prices. Your gift will also support transportation, storage and refrigeration of food.

Here's what your gift makes possible:

Donation	Meals served
$15	22
$25	36
$50	72
$100	144
$500	720

Send your Gift Today...

We'll use 95 cents of every dollar you give to support local food shelves. (Our fundraising costs are much less than many other organizations)

Emergency FoodShelf Network
1400 - 12th Avenue N.E.
Minneapolis, Minnesota 55413-1602

6 1 2 - 7 8 8 - 7 7 7 7

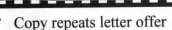

Copy repeats letter offer

---

1 out of 8 children is regularly hungry *

* Food Research and Action Center

Emergency FoodShelf Network:

For the last 15 years, Emergency FoodShelf Network, a coalition of 26 food shelves, has served the hungry in Hennepin County. We also enhance the capacity of member food shelves through the following services:

Economical food purchasing at bulk rates

Food transportation to site locations

Computer and management systems assistance

Cooperative fundraising

Food Shelf Locations

Minneapolis (19 sites)	Eden Prairie
New Hope	St. Louis Park
Richfield	Minnetonka
Crystal	Brooklyn Center

Hunger hurts

People of all ages. . .

Two-thirds of those served are children.

One-third of households using food shelves are working.

One-third of adults served have recently been laid off or are looking for work.

Ten percent of those served are senior citizens living on a fixed income.

"I tell them there is no more food to eat.....but they don't understand. I don't think any child ever understands."

Maria, parent

"All you can eat" doesn't mean much to some kids. . .

You can help provide food to the hungry. . .

Illustration 13-4: Emergency Foodshelf Direct Mail Reply Device

Reply device used for acquisition campaign

Yes ... I want to help the fight against hunger

Check boxes that apply

Here's my donation of : $20☐ $40☐ $75☐   Other ☐

Please charge my _____ Visa _____ MasterCard _____ Discover _____ Exp. date

Signature _____   Card Number _____

Check enclosed ☐

Thank you

ADDRESS BLOCK

Please fill in employer & phone number for matching gifts........and address changes.

Name _____
Address _____
City, State and Zip _____
Phone number _____
Employer, for matching gifts _____

Your contribution is tax-deductible to the extent allowed by law
Please make check payable to Emergency FoodShelf Network

Holiday Appeal

Yes. . . I want to help provide food to people in crisis

Please fill out below

Here's my donation of;   ☐ $50.00   ☐ Other _____

Please charge my _____ Visa _____ MasterCard _____ Exp. date _____
Signature _____ Card Number _____
Check inside _____

Thank you

Please note any changes, phone number, and employer for matching gifts
Name _____
Street, city, state, zip _____
Phone number _____
Employer (for matching gifts) _____
(Your employer may match your gift. We may need to call you

to fill out matching gift forms.)

ADDRESS BLOCK

Personalized gift "ask" reflects donor's last gift

Simple, low-cost and easy-to-produce reply device. Could be completed in-house in small numbers with merge-mail software.

Illustration 13-5: Emergency Foodshelf Network direct mail envelope

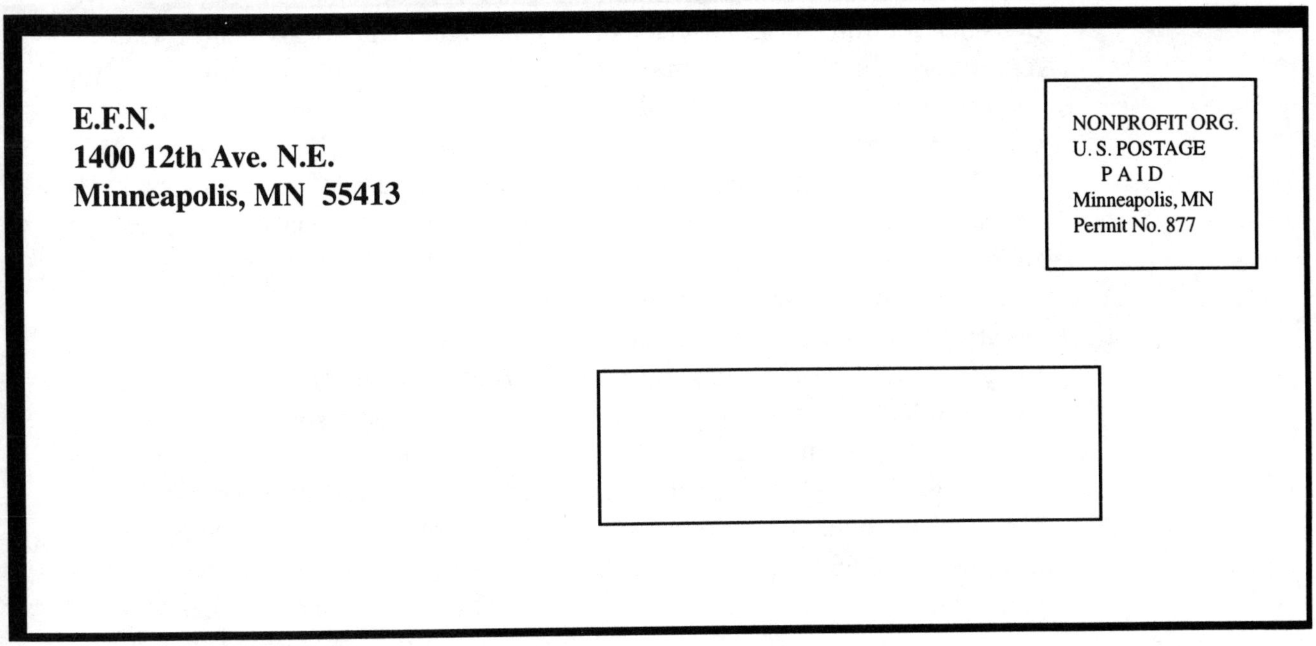

E.F.N.
1400 12th Ave. N.E.
Minneapolis, MN 55413

NONPROFIT ORG.
U. S. POSTAGE
P A I D
Minneapolis, MN
Permit No. 877

Donor/Member Segmentation Strategies

The success of the food shelf campaign was based on the premise that donors need to be treated in distinctly different ways, depending upon their relationship to the organization. In this manner, donors who are "close friends" and have been giving in larger amounts for a period of time will be treated like close friends. Highly personalized communications such as personal notes, letters, thank-you cards, or invitations are the proper collateral to cultivate the virtues of the friendship.

Similarly, donors who have broken the friendship through non-giving need to be encouraged through communications that reinforce or reintroduce the relationship, such as client stories or accomplishments that highlight the capability or need for the organization. Because these "friends" have distanced themselves from the organization, you may not wish to communicate as frequently. However, with consistent communication, "distant" friends or lapsed donors may move to a closer relationship with the organization through additional gift giving or volunteerism. When this happens, such a move should be appropriately acknowledged with a personal thank-you note.

Fund raising managers may believe that they lack the time to develop different communications for the various key publics. Another common objection from development managers not wanting to implement segmentation strategies is that the database is too small. It's true that effective segmentation requires analytical judgment of all of your key publics. However, it does not require you to change everything you are doing with all of these publics. Often the same communications vehicle, whether phone, mail or other, can be used, with minor adaptation. You then can add personalization or other special touches for the organization's "best friends." And, as you learned in Chapter 2, a good database program is essential to the entire process.

In our work and interviews with nonprofit development managers, we discovered that many managers do develop different communications for corporations and individual donors. However, few develop separate communications for distinct segments within the individual donor base, such as board members and volunteers.

When considering whether you should segment your database of publics, you should consider the following question: If you called a friend today whom you hadn't seen in five years, would you speak any differently to him or her than you would to your closest friend with whom you speak nearly every day? Most development professionals would probably answer yes. Yet how many actually segment their databases in order to speak to their various "friends" with similarly appropriate communications?

Each organization may wish to segment its database in a different way, depending on the size of the house file, the size of individual segments, and the goals of the marketing/fund raising program. For example, an organization with a small database of only 500 names may be in a better position to personalize all communications, as compared to an organization that has a house file of 20,000 names. Similarly, it is more productive to develop a larger campaign for a major gift segment of 1,000 names than to develop one for 25 names. At the same time, the development manager of a small database may wish to group similar segments whenever feasible. However, at all times, the development manager must keep in mind that communications for a major gift donor should appear more friendly, personal, and have a different tone and content than for the individual making a first gift to the organization.

In sum, a segmentation strategy should be customized for every organization. It should consider:

- The types of communications the organization uses: Is there a newsletter that transmits vital educational information? How often are telemarketing and mail solicitations used?

- The quantity of the house, or organizational file: Large data bases of 10,000 or more may require more segmentation because prioritizing communication messages may result in additional cost-savings when mailing in larger quantities. Conversely, the cost savings accrued when mailing to a file with less than 100 pieces is expected to be minimal.

- The interests of the donor or public segment: It's useful to know the source of a name, or how the name originally entered your file. However, it's not necessary to segment your entire database based on this sole criteria. Larger organizations with huge databases may wish to develop direct mail solicitations based on specific programs that donors have enrolled in or supported in the past. However, you may also find that donors who have participated in other programs will also donate to a new or different project.

- The quality and intensity of the relationship: More than any other criteria, this is the most important determinant for segmentation. Donors and volunteers who have committed significant time and or wealth to the organization want and need to be treated differently. Therefore, the quality of this relationship should be reinforced

The development manager must keep in mind that communications for a major gift donor should appear more friendly, personal, and have a different tone and content than for the individual making a first gift to the organization.

83

by special communications: first class mail, special invitations, personalized mail, and other types of communications normally reserved for special friends.

You may wish to consider designing the following segments for your house file:

■ Current donors;

■ LYBNT donors (last year but not the current year);

■ PYBNT donors (past years but not the current year);

■ Donors who give by phone;

■ Donors to special events;

■ Donors who give when receiving a premium;

■ Membership donors;

■ Board and committee members;

■ Volunteers;

■ Gift amount.

Now that you have an idea how to segment your database, here are a few examples to get you started in developing specific communication strategies for each segment:

■ A major donor segment: a personalized solicitation letter signed by the chairperson of the board.

■ New donors segment: a "welcome to the organization" package that includes a personal letter, program brochure, volunteer opportunities, and a donor return envelope.

■ A corporate donor segment: a letter from a corporate leader serving on your board, the annual report, updates on strategic planning, status reports of current grants and programs, positive testimonials, and reprints of articles relating to programs pertaining to the donor's interest.

Public Relations and the Board: Nine Easy Ideas

A thorough board orientation program is essential to the development of dedicated and effective board members. The first requisite is a detailed description of the requirements of their position addressing such questions as: Does this include making a financial contribution? Approximately how many hours will the board member be expected to volunteer? What duties should they be expected to perform?

This job description should be included along with a tour of the organization and a case statement that describes the organization's mission, target populations, programs, future strategies, and results. Additionally, you may wish to include a training session on gift cultivation and solicitation.

Improved communications with board members and continued recognition of their contributions to your organization are important ingredients in developing an active and committed board. You may wish to consider some type of public recognition. For example, board members who are independent business owners are among those who normally appreciate any positive publicity. Critical to making this happen, however, is that you have first obtained permission from the individual to use his or her name in a news release or feature story. This important first step allows individuals to retain their privacy, if desired.

Equally important is the question: If the organization recognizes one individual, how will others feel who go unrecognized? It is understandable to publicly recognize an outstanding board chair who has provided endless hours of service to an organization. It may also be appropriate to recognize, in a less public way, other committed board members. The opportunities for improved communications with your board, increased involvement of board members in your public relations activities, and free publicity that is available to highlight their contributions are only limited by your creativity. Here are nine easy ideas:

■ Mail a monthly letter from the executive director to the board updating them on program developments, special gifts, staffing changes, and any community recognition for your organization.

■ Send news clippings about your organization to board members and key volunteers.

■ Use board members as active participants in the organization's volunteer speaker's bureau.

■ Enlist board members as press and media contacts.

Improved communications with board members and continued recognition of their contributions to your organization are important ingredients in developing an active and committed board.

Illustration 14: Board Member Job Description

ABC ORGANIZATION

OBJECTIVE:

To serve as director of the board of ABC organization and to provide direction to the organization through the function of planning, evaluating, and policy setting.

ACCOUNTABILITY:

Organization Board President

QUALIFICATIONS:

Demonstrated interest in improving the lives of all children, youth, and families in the organization's jurisdiction. Specific skills and experience related to program, administration, personnel, finance management, resource development, or community relations. Representative of some aspect or segment of community population.

COMMITMENTS:

Willing to assume responsibility for corporate management of the organization.
Three-year term of office.
Approximately 8 hours per month.
Serve on at least one committee of the board.
Willing to make a personal financial commitment commensurate with ability to contribute.

RESPONSIBILITIES:

Ensure corporate management direction for the organization.
Ensure fulfillment of legal obligations.
Ensure provision of quality programs that extend ABC organization services to children, youth, and families throughout the jurisdiction.
Ensure that human resources of the organization are secured and managed.
Ensure that assets of the agency are prudently protected and managed.
Secure the funds necessary for the organization.
Secure community involvement and support.
Be knowledgeable of the operations of the organization.
Be knowledgeable of people, trends, and happenings in the community.
Attend and participate in all board and assigned committee meetings.
Represent ABC organization in the community as assigned.
Carry out assignments as delegated by the board president or committee chairperson.

- Write articles about your board members' accomplishments, then see that they are published in their company newsletters.

- Feature a board member in your newsletter or annual report.

- Ask a board member to write a donor appeal letter.

- Ask board members to write letters or call key donors to thank them for their gifts.

- Recognize a lead volunteer or key board member in the local news paper or community readerboard.

Public Relations and the Employee

Employees are excellent prospects for giving campaigns because they often possess more intimate knowledge about the organization and its mission. Frequently, however, development managers are reluctant to start an employee campaign because they believe that it will not be well accepted.

Similar to any campaign, the public relations aspect of an employee giving program must be considered. Each employee, depending on his or her role within the organization, has a different knowledge base about the organization and its mission. Therefore, it is the job of the development or public relations

manager to develop communications that ensure that all employees are aware of the key facts in the organization's case statement. These can be distributed to the employee in the first few days on the job. Or, if such a practice has not been used in the past, a half-day lunch seminar might be in order.

Managers at all levels may question resources for public relations and marketing communications that are directed to employees. However, managers must be encouraged to understand that nearly all employees communicate with the organization's key publics. Therefore, proper education and preparation will help the employee to more effectively promote the organization. Moreover, proper education will set the stage for future campaigns that will involve employees as spokespeople or contributors.

Employees can be cultivated as dedicated contributors. However, before launching an employee campaign you may wish to consider a key question: Are employees generally satisfied with working conditions? Many employees who work for nonprofit organizations accept lower wages than their private-based counterparts. Employees must feel that they are being treated fairly by their employer before they will consider contributing.

Additionally, an effective employee

Consider using the goal of 100 percent giving by staff as a means to kickoff a first-time staff campaign, rather than a specific dollar goal.

campaign has solid underpinnings in an organization whose culture encourages giving. Strong-arm tactics may work for the short term, but generally tend to build resentment. There are many options that will encourage a strong culture of employee giving. You may consider a recognition program to honor employees whose example represents a generous spirit of giving. Consider a humorous newsletter feature story, a commendation plaque for the first 1000 hours of volunteer project time, or a photo of an employee donating a portion of his or her paycheck. You may also wish to consider asking another employee to develop the employee recognition materials. Many employees enjoy honoring others and might enjoy an opportunity to be creative.

Whatever public relations activities you choose, they should be timed for maximum exposure prior to the start of the campaign, and continuing until the campaign conclusion.

Other factors are important to remember. Plan around pay periods, when you are not competing with other fund raising appeals. Consider using the goal of 100 percent giving by staff as a means to kickoff a first-time staff campaign, rather than a specific dollar goal.

Make it easy for employees to give. Options such as payroll deductions, cash gifts, credit card charges, and

electronic fund transfer programs are just as attractive to your fellow employees as they are to other donors. Lastly, like other donors, employees like to be thanked and recognized for their gifts.

Public Relations and Your External Publics

Effective Crisis Management

Many fine books outline how to implement creative public relations programs. Yet one of the most critical aspects of public relations, one that can seriously affect your organization, is often overlooked in many public relations plans: crisis management. It is important to realize that every organization could face a crisis capable of adversely affecting its functioning for many years to come.

The types of crises may differ, as well as their respective responses. Above all, it is important to remember that even though such a crisis may never affect your organization, it is nonetheless imperative that you plan for its occurrence.

Consider the following case of the United Way. Although many factors, including board stewardship were at play here, the case example clearly illustrates a crisis situation that could have been prevented, or at least minimized with public relations pre-planning.

Case Example

In 1991, a public relations crisis occurred for United Way. It was discovered that the highest-ranking official of the United Way, William Arimony, was suspected of mismanagement of funds. Various spokespeople from the United Way attempted to quell the negative press that developed. However, it was clear to public relations professionals, that no crisis management systems were in place to adequately address the significant and momentous events that had occurred during Arimony's tenure.

An audit of the organization was promised, as board members attempted to justify financial operations that had repeatedly seemed to favor the well-being of the executive director. Excessive pay and perks, including air travel, automobiles, and other personal benefits, were discovered.

Many months transpired before the full extent of the issues was clarified. Unfortunately, the impact of this public relations fiasco went far beyond involvement at the national level. United Way fund raising campaigns at local levels across the nation were severely impacted. During 1991-1992, funds raised by local United Way chapters fell by 4.1%. Even worse, shortfalls at the national level resulted in the organization being unable to make payroll.

Perhaps most disheartening was that the effects of this fiasco traveled well beyond the involvement of United Way agencies. Executive compensation became the watchword for board members throughout the country, as more and more individuals became aware of the issues surrounding compensation packages for nonprofit employees. The public also began to question if funds were being used effectively by nonprofit organizations of all types.

Perhaps it is unfair to blame the negative snowballing of this single episode on the United Way. Yet, after this event, the general public became more clearly aware that nonprofit organizations were not beyond reproach. After all, if the public trust could be damaged by one of the most respected charities in America, what more could be expected from other nonprofit groups?

As we consider these momentous events, we must recognize the necessity of pre-planning for disaster or crisis management: to intercept negative opinion before it accelerates out of control. Today, Elaine Chao, United Way executive, has a public relations plan that has begun to achieve positive media relations for the organization. Feature stories in several national publications continue to chart the organization's restructuring, strict operational controls, and vigorous recovery from past losses.

As you put together your organization's public relations and marketing plan, consider a number of possible crisis scenarios. Although every organization uniquely determines what constitutes a possible crisis, the *response* to a crisis is consistently similar for all organizations. The first step in crisis management is to attempt to foresee what situation would be considered an emergency for your organization.

Some possible crisis situations might include:

■ Confidential client information that suddenly becomes public;

■ Wrong-doing of a key employee;

■ Injury or death of a program participant;

■ Misuse of an organization's funds;

■ A world event that threatens your organization's key publics;

■ A government law that is enacted that severely impacts your organization's key publics.

Once you have identified some possible crisis situations, you will be in a position to plan your response. You may wish to consider:

What Staff Would Be Appointed to Handle the Crisis?

An organization must avoid a situation where any staff member, board member, or volunteer is allowed to respond publicly, with their own personal interpretation, when questioned about the crisis.

Rather, every organization should appoint a key spokesperson or spokespeople who will respond when needed. The role of the spokesperson(s) must be known and accepted by all within the organization. It is also very important to reconfirm this assignment on an annual basis. Often, small crises develop into larger ones because of the mismanagement or miscommunication of information. This can be avoided by selecting the right individual(s) to communicate important messages during the crisis period. Your key spokesperson(s) should be someone who is close enough to the organization to understand its needs. He or she should be an individual who can communicate confidence and respect. Above all, this individual should be available to respond in timely fashion. Often the key spokesperson for an organization is the director of communications or the executive director.

What Key Messages Would You Use to Disquiet Public Outcry or to Restore Public Confidence?

You may wish to explain to the public what staff would be appointed to handle the situation, including their credentials, and specific steps that will result in a solution to the problem or potential problems. In this manner, the public can be made aware of the efficacy of your organization. You can turn around a potentially explosive situation into a situation that promotes your effectiveness as an organization.

How Will You Deliver Key Messages?

Part of your public relations plan should include what media will be used to deliver the messages. Will you use radio, television, or press releases to print media? As well, you will want to specify, to the extent possible, the specific audiences that should be targeted.

Preventive and Proactive Public Relations that Prevent Crisis

News reporters are always looking for good stories. Because they are entrusted with submitting truthful information with fact and detail, they often rely upon the testimony of experts. Your organization may be in the perfect position to provide expert opinion to the press and broadcast media.

Consider making yourself the expert in an area of importance. You can provide backgrounders to the media on a regular basis. Backgrounders are reports that give factual information about a topic of interest. An international relief organization may wish to provide backgrounders that discuss the political climate in the countries in which it operates. As news develops in these countries, reporters may call you to discuss pertinent facts.

By initiating and building relationships with the media, you are practicing preventive public relations. Often, when negative publicity is developing, astute news reporters will call their sources, or contacts, before issuing any publicity. This gives you the opportunity to address any misunderstandings before damage ensues.

Public Relations: How the Media Can Improve Your Image and Results

The next important step in your public relations campaign is to develop the strategy to motivate your publics to action. Key factors that will determine the feasibility of the campaign are your human and financial resources. Campaigns can be developed at varying degrees of intensity. In implementing your public relations plan, you will need to consider whether you can obtain your expected outcome with currently available resources.

Current research indicates that for a new campaign or a new program, it often takes an average of six to seven exposures (or frequencies) for a message to actually reach the conscious mind of the target audience. This means that your target public will have to see or hear your message a minimum of seven times before performing the desired behavior.

Mature organizations, or projects that have already received some past publicity, may need fewer exposures in order to accomplish the same goal. For example, in order to reach your target public, a new organization may have to appear in a newspaper three or four times, on the radio five to six times, on flyers or bulletins that blanket the area, or any other combination of exposures. The number of exposures necessary will be influenced by: (1) how many people you wish to influence, (2) the geographic area you wish to cover, and (3) their present attitudes and knowledge.

Implementing a public relations campaign is a time-consuming and detail-oriented job. Fortunately, most nonprofit managers will discover many resources right in their own community to help them manage a public relations campaign. Advertising agencies or marketing firms are often looking for projects that will allow them to use their creativity in new ways while boosting a worthy cause. Many are interested in the additional visibility of a public relations project.

You may locate possible pro-bono sources by: (1) contacting corporate volunteer/human resource offices, (2) publishing notices in a company's newsletter to locate specific staff, (3) calling your local advertising council or public relations and/or advertising professional societies, or (4) calling a business directly. This recruitment process might take a few months. Your prospective volunteer candidate will want to know more about the project, its purpose and budget, and your organization's mission, history, and capabilities. Volunteer candidates may also need approval from their employers before they agree to staff or support a pro-bono project. If you are lucky, you may be able to recruit an entire team, including an art director, copy writer, and account executive, all from one agency.

Once your volunteer team is in place, you will also need to secure the human and financial resources to implement the campaign. A volunteer and/or intern may serve as your internal manager for the project. Or, you may delegate the project to a marketing/public relations committee, under the supervision of one key volunteer. When delegating this responsibility, you may wish to

Media Protocols

Date: August 10, 1996

Craftings **Campaign**
To: all volunteers, committee chairs and key spokespeople
From: Diane Hodiak, publicity chair

Strategy

Volunteers and staff will seek to increase visibility of the events of Craftings '96, thereby encouraging public participation and establishing a positive image for the organizations and artists associated with the project.

Messages

Craftings is a week-long celebration of the crafts industry in the Pacific Northwest Region. Activities include: Pioneer Square Gallery Tours of the crafts of Northwest Artisans, Designer Fashion Show by Friends of the Cloth, and a workshop at Seattle Center, the Crafts and Business Exchange, which is specially designed for craftspeople. Because this workshop is priced so moderately, it is possible for anyone to attend. ($10 for the 3-day session.) This is possible because of the sponsorship of local business, local arts groups and the National Endowment for the Arts.

Protocols

In an effort to maintain consistent communications to the public, volunteer and staff are requested to direct all media calls to the following individuals:

> Charles Sheena, Publicity Chair
> Anne Divan, Executive Director, Allied Artisans

All calls should be handled as quickly as possible.
Specific questions about any particular arts organizations should be directed to the specific organization. The list of participating organizations and their phone numbers is included with this release.

consider the following questions:

■ Does the key volunteer manager have a clear understanding of the mission, history, and image that your organization seeks to promote?

A useful tool for training volunteers is the protocol sheet. This identifies the key strategies and objectives of the campaign, and states them in such a way that they are easily understood. A protocol sheet also contains sample messages to be used with the media. Once participants are made aware of key messages and strategies for the campaign, their job is made much easier. Another consideration is that if volunteers are new to your organization, they will need additional background materials to build their base of knowledge.

■ Do the key volunteers have the dedication and attention to detail that is necessary to write the press releases, mail them, and complete follow-up phone calls?

■ What can volunteers realistically be expected to do, given their training and knowledge?

■ Will you, as a staff member, be the media contact, or will a board member be involved?

These details can make or break a campaign. Above all, you will want to make sure that these key people will present a favorable image for your organization. Alternatively, if you personally don't feel comfortable before a radio or television audience, then it may be better for you to delegate this task to someone who thrives in the limelight. Remember, good management includes effective delegation, when necessary.

The sample protocol sheet is shown in Illustration 15.

Simple Steps for Effective Media Relations

How to Develop a Press Kit

A press kit is a folder with all pertinent information about a media campaign. The contents may vary for each project but can include:

■ Cover or exterior folder with rapid identification logo or slogan;

■ Press release with name of contact person;

■ Media advisory letter;

■ Feature story idea sheet;

■ Personal biographies of key celebrities or participants;

- Organization's annual report;

- Photos of key figures;

- Posters, brochures;

- Local information (particularly important for national publicity);

- Timeline of events or activities;

- News clippings or excerpts from publications about the key facts;

- Sample audio tape or video.

Note: all pieces in the kit should contain the contact name and phone number, in case any of the pieces are misplaced. An explanation follows for the press release and media advisory letter, the two most commonly used pieces.

The Press Release

The press or news release addresses the five Ws of advertising: who, what, when, where, and why. Because editors and news staff are busy individuals, you want to provide a strong lead sentence in the press release, providing the five W's of information as soon as possible in the release. A # is used at the end of the release to indicate the end of the document.

The Media Advisory Letter

The media advisory letter is used for a variety of purposes. It can be used to introduce a packet of information that will be arriving at a later date. Often the media advisory letter serves as an announcement, or introduction for a large campaign or media event. The purpose of the media advisory letter will determine the content of the letter. However, you will most commonly use it to provide a background, summary, announcement, or introduction.

When to Mail Your Press Kit

Radio, print, and television media all have different lead times for submission of publicity materials. Generally, television requires the longest (generally one to six months), and radio and print the shortest (one week to two months). An advance phone call to the producer, editor, or administrative services for the station or network will usually yield information about required lead times.

Except in the case of breaking news, when you must be timely with your announcement, you will need to send your press kit well in advance of lead times so that it can be considered for placement. By doing this you have a greater chance of securing publicity on the appropriate shows and program specials, when it is most advantageous for your campaign.

Research indicates that your target public will have to see or hear your message several times before they will perform the desired behavior.

The ability to achieve coverage in print and broadcast media...is the result of having a newsworthy story that is effectively promoted to the right media contacts.

Unfortunately, it is not uncommon for media personnel to lose your press kit. Some individuals have efficient systems that organize factual information. More frequently than not, however, your press kit, or parts of its contents, will become lost in the great media Bermuda Triangle known as the "media dump." For this reason, it's wise to prepare extra copies to re-send to media once it is closer to the actual lead and campaign dates.

Media contacts receive so many press kits that it can be difficult for them to remember one from another. For this reason, many marketers develop creatively designed and eye-catching materials to aid recognition.

Following Up with the Right People: the Key to Success

A key ingredient to the success of your publicity campaign is knowing *who* to contact. Contrary to popular opinion, the ability to achieve coverage in print and broadcast media is not related to how many "friends" you have in the media. Rather, it is the result of having a newsworthy story that is effectively promoted to the right media contacts.

There are a few standards for you to consider, recognizing that each radio, television, or print media operation is different. Depending upon the size, ownership, and mission of the media entity, jobs can be designed quite

differently. Your best strategy may be to ask for the name of the editor or reporter who covers stories in your topic area. Usually, media personnel are happy to assist callers in finding the right party. Generally, you can use the following guidelines to help you locate the right individual:

- **News stations**: assignment editor, further defined as morning, evening and weekend assignment editors;

- **Television programs or features**: producer;

- **Public service announcements:** director of public or community affairs;

- **Radio programs:** program director, or, for a news item, the news director;

- **Newswires:** reporters for specialized stories; otherwise for smaller shops, the editor or bureau chief;

- **Newspapers**: reporter who covers topics similar to yours (Although an editor will make the final decision as to what copy is included, the reporter is still your best contact to get the story written).

One of the more challenging jobs in public relations is maintaining a current media personnel list. This is an

Illustration 16: Press Release

Craftings '96
107 South Bradford
Seattle, WA 98104
206-624-0432

September 1, 1996
Subject: *The Crafts Exchange*
From: Diane Hodiak   206-525-8933 fax 206-525-8934

The first of its kind in the Pacific Northwest, *The Crafts Exchange* will provide "how-to" information in grand style. This workshop, presented as part of **Craftings '96,** will be held October 3-5 at the Seattle Center where all can attend for a registration fee of $10.

Designed to bring the crafts and business community together, events for DAY l of the workshop include keynote speaker Bruce Bean, famous marketing expert. A panel discussion featuring key figures from government, craft and business communities will be moderated by Michael Patrick, author of the *Crafts Business Guide.* DAY 2 will be devoted to sales and marketing, where traditional outlets of whole-sale, retail, consignment, and commissions will be discussed. Promotional techniques will be taught as well as a special segment on how to present your slide show or portfolio.DAY 3 will feature how to manage a business, including accounting, taxes, insurance, artist's rights and selling on consignment.

Interested parties may register at the event, or by calling Allied Artisans, at 206-666-7856. Entrants may participate in all or any number of the daily sessions.

The *Crafts Exchange* is presented as part of **Craftings '96,** a regional celebration of the crafts which is funded in part by Seattle, King County, and Washington Arts Commissions, local business, National Endowment for the Arts, and Allied Artisans.

Illustration 16; Media Advisory Letter

Craftings '96
107 South Bradford
Seattle, WA 98104
206-624-0432

Media Advisory

Nelson Avery, Arts Editor   September 5, 1996
Seattle Times
400 Union Street
Seattle, WA 98100

Dear Nelson Avery,

This coming October 3-5, *Craftings '96,* a week-long celebration of the Crafts of the Northwest, will feature several activities for local artists, art businesses, and art enthusiasts. Activities will include the Craft Exchange, a workshop designed to provide business expertise to the art community, a family hands-on art workshop, a crafts exhibit, and an exotic fashion show of wearable art.

The fashions show will feature one-of-a-kind outfits, designed by local textile artisans. These creations are truly a visual spectacle, with their unique costuming and long colored weavings and fabrics. The show will be held on October 4, at the Seattle Pavilion at 7 P.M. Two complimentary tickets are enclosed.

Moderator for the fashion show is Gina Jackson, notable northwest fabric artist. Unlike other fashion shows, Gina will provide commentary on the intricate makings of these unusual costumes. Artists will also be on hand to discuss their work and offer tours of artist's spaces at later, prearranged times.

Equally exciting is the workshop planned for families. Several outstanding local artists will appear at Seattle Center in the plaza area to lead craft activities in clay, paper, and textiles. Families are sure to appreciate these offerings that are free of charge.

Together, more than 22 outstanding artists will display their handicrafts at this show. Never before has the Northwest had such a comprehensive display of local crafts. If you would be interested in interviewing any of these talented artists, I would be pleased to help you with the arrangements. I have enclosed three biographies and photos of their unusual wearable art.

Other information about *Craftings '96* activities is enclosed.

Sincerely,

Diane Hodiak
Publicity Coordinator   206-525-8933   fax; 206-525-8934

industry where there is continual change and reorganization. To address this ever-present need, media service companies have entered the marketplace for the purpose of compiling current lists for different types of contacts.

Many major cities have media service companies that provide a complete list of services from identification of publication type to contact person. These companies will also complete the entire mailing (or faxing) according to your detailed specifications. Media services have comprehensive lists from the international level down to the detailed selection of editors and managers for specific publications and broadcast media.

Still, it's wise to remember that although these services provide contact names, these names may not actually be your correct contact. The real advantage of using these services is that they save you time by providing you with names and addresses you may not otherwise have available. They also provide additional services, such as photo duplication and mail preparation, which you may not be able to handle during a peak business time.

Before using these services you may wish to ask:

- Will the service provide appropriate names that would take me a long time to compile?

- Will the service help to complete a press mailing in timely fashion? Sometimes this alone is well worth the expense.

- Do I have sufficient staff and/or volunteers to implement a large press mailing?

- Is the cost of services more economical for certain jobs? For example, if they have a relationship with a photo supplier, perhaps they may be able to duplicate your photos for less than you could at your local photo shop.

If you wish to compile your own database of media contacts, you can use the resource publication *Bacon's Guide to Broadcast and Print Media,* in the reference section of your local library. This guide is published yearly and lists many of the major media across the United States. Bacon's also provides names and associated media services. Their phone number is 1-800-621-0561.

Further, if you wish to develop more personalized contacts, you may find them simply by calling your local radio or television stations and by reading your local newspaper.

In the print media, reporters, like other professionals, have areas of expertise. Depending on the size of

You will significantly increase the amount of free publicity you receive if you follow up with personal phone calls to people after you have sent them your press kit.

the paper, there may be one or several reporters, each specializing in human interest stories, medical stories, or other topic areas. If you're still in doubt after reading several issues, you can call the newspaper to ask who might handle topics related to your news item. Reporters often work with the pressures of deadlines, but are still willing to refer contacts to the right reporter when necessary.

Now that you know *who* to contact, you will significantly increase the amount of free publicity you receive if you follow up with personal phone calls to these people after you have sent them your press kit. Before you call, however, it's best to prepare a sales presentation.

It is courteous to ask if your key person is on deadline. Media people continually manage deadlines, and may be preoccupied with a story when you make your first contact. If this is the case, it's better to call back later at a prearranged time. If they are available, be prepared to make your pitch in 20 seconds or less.

You might say: "This is Sally Smith from Blue Mountain Theater Group. We're hosting a ball that will be attended by John Pratt, one of Chicago's biggest names in jazz. I'd like to let you know that we have one activity planned that would be very visually exciting for television (This is always important for television.) I have already sent you our materials.

Would you be interested in covering the event?"

If they are not interested, then try to discover the reason. Have they covered the topic before? Are there too many similar events in your community? Once you know the reason, you can adequately address it as an objection. You might also ask if there is anyone else who might cover the event, or ask if they would consider doing some coverage for a different activity. Even though their response might seem lukewarm, your detailed questions might be able to stir interest in some other aspect of the campaign. Or, you may procure their interest and thereby obtain some type of coverage for future activities.

Conducting the Interview

At last! You are scheduled to appear on an important talk show. What do you do next?

Above all, always remember to bring your pertinent materials with you, even if you have already sent them in advance. You don't want to be in the position of needing one of your key props and not have it available. If you want to use a visual, let the producer of the show know in advance. Visuals are often welcomed, if they are of adequate quality for broadcasting. Photos, slides, film clips, books, audio tapes and videotapes can all be used, depending upon the equipment

GREENFIELD PUBLIC LIBRARY
7215 WEST COLDSPRING RD
GREENFIELD, WI 53220

available at the studio.

Some interviewers prepare for weeks in order to interview an important personality. Barbara Walters has been known to conduct extensive research on her key subjects. However, this is the exception rather than the rule. The best way to prepare your interviewer is to compose a list of questions in advance. This allows you to present your key information and makes the interviewer's work easier. Moreover, with a supplied list of questions, you can lead the discussion to points or issues that favorably represent your strategic messages.

You will need approximately 7-9 questions for a 15-minute interview or pro-rated per fraction thereof. If there are others being interviewed as part of the same program, of course the amount of air time you receive will be substantially less. Additionally, you will appear in a more favorable light if you also consider answers to possible interview questions *in advance*.

There are times, however, when the interviewer will want to develop the question format. In this event, you still have the right to know the topics and scope of the interview. They should tell you how long the interview will last, and if there will be additional questions allowed by a studio or call-in audience.

The Print Media

It *is* possible to obtain free advertising in some publications. Most commonly, smaller newspapers will offer free space on an "as-available" basis. Larger metropolitan newspapers are less likely to offer space because they usually have plenty of paid advertisers.

The disadvantage of using free space is that you are not guaranteed to receive space in a particular issue. This makes planning difficult. Also, publications will not want to provide you with free space if they know that you are a paying customer in another publication.

Thus, although free advertising space is an excellent option, you must exercise this option with care. If you have an advertising budget, it may be best to negotiate lower rates rather than to negotiate free space with one provider and then pay for space with another. This creates hard feelings among advertisers and may minimize your chances of receiving free publicity when you really need it, such as a feature article or cover story.

Additionally, there are many other options for free and low-cost publicity, such as event calendars. Printed publications provide event information as a service to subscribers and are generally hungry for this information. Also, check to see if your local newspapers have a volunteer opportunity section. These are good opportunities for free advertising for position openings.

Newspaper Feature Articles

Feature articles provide the most visible free publicity. Feature articles are easily obtained for newsworthy topics. You can increase your chances of obtaining a feature article by sending out press releases on new or interesting ideas or happenings at your organization.

If you wish to try to secure free publicity through a newspaper feature article, it's best to send your press release or press kit along with a media advisory letter. Your points of contact may be the reporters who have bylines in your target newspaper.

As we mentioned earlier, in larger metropolitan newspapers, reporters will each normally follow a particular topic for the paper. Many become experts in a certain field, such as medical research, human interest, or foundation or nonprofit news. By finding out which reporter is most likely to handle the stories you are proposing, you are more likely to get your story placed.

If a volunteer or other stakeholder will be interviewed, it is wise to brief them on the protocol sheet mentioned earlier in this chapter. Additionally,

For media interviews remember the rule of three: tell them what you want them to know, tell them again, and then tell them again!

you should furnish the reporter with a printed reference sheet including key dates, the spelling of the names of your organization and its staff, and other key information used in the article. This ensures more accuracy by the reporter.

Also, remember the rule of three: tell them what you are going to tell them, tell them again, and then tell them again in conclusion. Naturally one needs to be creative in portraying these messages so that they do not appear repetitious. Nonetheless, through the repetition of related themes, key strategic messages will be clearly communicated.

Whether you or another individual will be the interviewee, you must develop protocols for the presentation. Remember that when communicating with the media, it is critically important to present clear and consistent messages. If you are presenting a difficult topic, try to break it down so that it is more easily understood. Use examples, if possible. This minimizes the likelihood that a reporter will misinterpret a statement or concept.

If you don't want to be the media contact, delegate this task to an individual who can speak with authority and who portrays a positive image. Inform them of the protocols for the interview.

Letters to the Editor

Nearly every newspaper and magazine features a section that invites comments from readers about past editorials, feature stories, or important topics of current interest. Many nonprofit managers and executives have received recognition in the letters to the editor section. These articles can discuss the details pertaining to a story about a select population that may or may not have been accurately portrayed. Or, you may offer a counter position to that which has already been represented. At the end of the story you will have the opportunity to display your name and organization, adding further credibility to your opinions.

This is not an opportunity to extol the virtues of your organization. Rather, its purpose is to remind readers about issues and facts, from a personal or professional point of view. The use of a catchy headline, however, will bring the reader into the story, and will enable you to promote your cause in subtle ways. Some publications prefer that you mark your piece at the top of the page with a separate line that identifies the topic discussed, and whether it is a counterpoint to an article that has already appeared.

Designing Cost Effective Marketing Communications

A solid public relations program includes many types of communications materials, each designed for cost-effectiveness. Certain types of communications are so expensive that they feasibly cannot be used for all audiences. These may include video presentations, annual reports, or special campaign folders.

One way to trim costs in marketing communications is to ensure that you are using the right type of communication for each of your key publics. In other words, you want to use your most expensive communications where they are most useful. For example, a board member or major donor is more likely to read a long brochure or report.

You may wish to consider evaluating your present marketing communications as well as how they are being delivered to see if you could minimize your costs. The following methods will provide you with some ideas to get started in cutting costs and targeting your communications:

■ Include a response card/evaluation form when appropriate: Would they like to continue receiving the communication? Do they consider it worthwhile?

■ When it fits your purposes,

One way to trim costs in marketing communications is to ensure that you are using the right type of communication for each of your key publics.

design several different communication pieces with similar colors and/or papers. In this way a printer can "gang" these pieces, or print them together from the same sheet of paper or with the same ink color. Depending on the job, this could save you up to several hundred dollars in paper and print costs.

■ Consider using the same communication vehicle, but in a minimized version.

■ Consider pre-printing a shell for your newsletter with just your key color, then add the black or one-color text at later dates. This will allow you to print in quantity, saving as much as 20 percent in printing costs.

Further, if your office copy machine will accept the paper you use, you may be able to copy the black text onto the pre-printed shells for each issue. (This is usually useful only if you are printing in smaller quantities, or have separate newsletters in smaller quantities for several target audiences.) If you have volunteers who can help you, it will increase your cost-savings.

■ Consider changing the vehicle of communication. Cable television and major print media can be extremely cost effective for large audiences. Internet capabilities

are extremely low-cost and useful when you can target the appropriate constituencies (see Chapter 3, Technology.)

Changing your marketing communications requires the courage to make mistakes. More often than not, however, you will find that if you are responding to donor or member needs, the benefits far outweigh the risks involved.

Ideas for Low-cost Marketing Communications

Next, we'll discuss some additional marketing communication vehicles to increase your organization's visibility and the number of exposures to the public eye. Consider these as supplementary materials to your brochures, annual reports, and donor communications.

Grocery/Discount Stores

Some grocery stores will allow nonprofit organizations to print advertisements on the sides of their paper grocery bags. This is an excellent way to reach people in a defined geographic area to promote your organization's programs or upcoming special events. Of course, if there is more than one store, then additional geographic reach is obtained. The exposure potential can be significant in a large metropolitan area comprising hundreds of thousands of individuals.

The store manager or publicity or marketing director will usually decide whether to charge for this service. Most frequently, there is no charge. In fact, the only work you will need to do is call in advance (often six to eight months) and prepare the camera-ready artwork to be printed on the bags.

Additional marketing ideas available through grocery stores are the smaller advertisements printed on tape receipts and the ad cards that appear on shopping carts. These are usually not sold by the store, but by a local or national media company. You may wish to inquire about these alternatives as well.

Display Advertising

Every city usually has one or more suppliers of billboard display advertising. Additionally, shopping malls, airports, bus shelters, and transit shelters offer message boards and kiosks to promote your message. Billboards allow you to promote an upcoming event, inform the public of your programs or services, or educate the viewer about the need for your organization's programs.

Additionally, billboards are an excellent means to reach large audiences and provide multiple exposures to your message. Some nonprofit organizations gain excellent exposure from display advertising at little cost to the marketing budget. The disadvantages are that you may not be able to select the audience who sees your message, choose the desired geographical penetration or best locations, or extend the time frame needed for your campaign. Additionally, optimum readability for billboards requires the use of only a few words. Therefore, the intensity or depth of your message is minimized. Despite these limitations, however, billboards can serve your purpose well.

Depending on the time of year and the location of the billboard, there may be selected off- months when billboards are less likely to be rented. It is during this down time that a billboard company will most likely allow a nonprofit organization to have free display advertising space.

In order to arrange for billboard space, you should usually inquire with the company's ad or public service representative. Because billboards are often rented months in advance, you will need to call a minimum of two to three months prior to the time slot you desire. You should also allow time for the printing of your billboard *slick*— the advertisement which is actually papered on the board itself.

Before deciding to go ahead with a display advertising project you will need to obtain an estimate as to how

During slow periods, display advertising companies often provide nonprofit organizations with free advertising space.

much you will need to spend to produce the ad materials. Although some billboard companies will pay for this, they most generally will want the nonprofit organization or sponsor to incur this cost. Depending on how many colors you use and the number of billboards, this cost may range from $300 to $2000. The public service or marketing director at the company may help you to determine your costs. This individual will probably be very happy that their billboard will be used every month, rather than sitting vacant. Billboard time is usually scheduled by the 30-day period.

While most companies will not guarantee a certain location, they frequently know which locations are most common for public service use. For example, locations that are tucked away in low visibility areas are most frequently available for public service use. Of course, these locations are less apt to be rented. However, opportunities do exist for high visibility locations if you can be flexible in your timing. In addition to location, a wide variety of different style boards may be available, including lighted, mechanical, and painted.

In sum, in order to use display advertising effectively, you need to (1) determine your target audience; (2) consider the goals of your marketing campaign; (3) evaluate how display advertising fits with other activities or exposures that are part of the campaign; (4) consider the suitability of specific billboard locations in accomplishing your communication goals; and (5) ask the outdoor display advertising company for estimates of traffic volume at specific locations.

Statement Stuffers

High-volume mailers such as department stores or cable and utility companies will sometimes allow inserts by nonprofit organizations to be included with monthly statements to consumers. When using statement stuffers, it's wise to know the mailing audience as well as the geographic location. Frequently, however, major mailers often have their own inserts, so you will need to contact them a few months in advance to inquire about availability. You will find that certain seasons of the year are busier than others, such as pre-holiday months.

Readerboards

Banks, community centers, and shopping centers generally have electronic readerboards that are available, without charge to nonprofit organizations, for items of public interest.

Usually these businesses will allow nonprofit organizations to use a portion of the signage for a period of time, from one to thirty days, depend-

ing on competition from other organizations and events in the community. The key to effective readerboard usage is to condense your message in catchy phrases so that passing motorists or pedestrians will have time to view it and remember it. You may wish to repeat key items such as dates and phone numbers.

Bulletins at Places of Worship

A printed bulletin in a church, synagogue, or other place of worship provides an excellent opportunity to promote a special event or funding appeal to an audience that may have special interest in your organization's mission. These communication vehicles may be used one time or over a period of weeks. Again, plan ahead and allow for enough lead time to get permission to place your communication, write the copy, and have the message printed in the bulletin.

Company and Association Newsletters

Most companies will gladly advertise volunteer opportunities for their employees and often print other messages in support of nonprofit organizations' events and services as well. Written copy and photos may be requested by the corporate communications office. If you have a key volunteer within a company, you may wish to make them the contact for

implementing your campaign at that level.

Shopping Center Signs

Perhaps your local shopping center has a lighted display with several panels, or they may have two-sided signs on free-standing metal stands. Ask if you can set up your own stand in another part of the center. Banks are also good places to put free-standing signs because they receive fairly heavy traffic at certain times of the month. The portable signs can also be set up at apartment and office complexes.

Movie Theaters

A few years ago, selected movie theaters donated the first few minutes before movie previews for information on nonprofit organizations. Today, as more and more marketers agree to pay for such time, the amount of space available at no cost is declining. Nonetheless, if you have slides suitable for movie theater usage, you may wish to try this idea. Many theaters offer special discount rates to nonprofit organizations. You may wish to consider this marketing opportunity to reach a large, captive audience with your message.

Rental Video Tapes

Increasingly, nonprofit organizations are using the pre-movie section on movie video cassettes to promote their message. This works especially well if the film on the video cassette is related to the theme of your communication (for example, an environmental organization may choose to advertise its programs and services on the lead that appears before a nature film.)

Piggy-Backing on Others' Promotions

If a company in your area is launching a large promotion, ask them if you can add an insert to their mailings, brochures, flyers, or other marketing collateral. Even if you can insert only a tag line or slogan, it will give you some additional exposure.

Another idea is to ask exhibitors at a trade show to display your brochures. This is second best to actually having a booth at a trade show. This works most effectively when your promotion goals correspond to the marketer's. If your organization prevents crime and violence, perhaps you might choose a company that sells burglar alarms.

This is where your creativity will shine. Consider possible connections between your organization and the company. Do you have a product or service that will serve their marketing target? Will it serve the company's interest too? In order to find out what companies are doing, consult your local city business newspapers or business sections of major news media.

Packaging Promotion

Would your campaign messages fit well on a marketer's own product packaging? This works best when you can actually approach a corporation that is already providing you with funding. In other words, *they know you and believe in you.* Think about the possible ways you can achieve a fit.

If you're an environmental organization, perhaps they have some packaging that is made with recyclable materials. This indicates that they might be interested in environmental issues. Or, if your organization serves children, then perhaps a product that is purchased by parents and used by children would enable both you and your marketing partner to attract your audiences at the same time. The Children's Miracle Network has been very successful and effective in using product packaging to promote their annual fund raising program.

Stadium Scoreboards

Electronic scoreboards at major sports stadiums allow you to present your message to large, captive audiences. Most professional sports teams will provide this service at no charge to nonprofit organizations who want to promote an upcoming event or an educational message. For instance, a local orchestra or museum may promote its upcoming 5K benefit run, or a civic organization may encourage spectators to become volunteers in a childhood literacy program. Your message may be displayed several times during the sporting event and reach audiences of tens of thousands of people who are keeping their eyes on the scoreboard.

In smaller communities, local stadiums and arenas may also offer similar opportunities. Although electronic scoreboards may not be available, local sports teams may allow your organization to display messages on a stationary sign near the scoreboard. This often provides high visibility during the game. The announcer may also be willing to promote your event or programs during game intermissions.

Mass Transit

Mass transit provides opportunities for your organization to use mobile billboards on buses, subways, and trains. Your message displayed on the side of a bus or on a display card within a subway or train is seen by thousands of people each day. Your message will travel to a number of different parts of a city or locality where it will be viewed by many people.

This form of promotion can be used effectively to promote an upcoming special event, to encourage donor support, or to educate the public on an issue which your organization is addressing through its programs and services.

Community mass transit programs also often offer special advertising rates to local nonprofit organizations. Your small development program may be able to find a corporate sponsor who will underwrite the cost of a display ad as their contribution to your program.

Cable Television

Cable television offers an affordable means for nonprofit organizations to present their mission, programs, services, and need for support to viewing audiences in their community. Public cable networks are required to offer community access channels that provide air time as well as studios for the editing and production of your presentations.

Cable networks provide an excellent opportunity to target certain geographic areas of the city, since large metropolitan areas often have several channels serving the area.

Another valuable service is that public cable networks often offer training in the use of their equipment. At some locations you may also find staff available to do your project for a reasonable fee.

Some stations do not allow solicitations to be aired on the station, but you can often complete a short video production that is suitable for fund raising and then add your actual solicitation request at a later time, after the product has been aired on the network.

Videotape Productions

Videotape productions offer small development programs an ideal way to get their message before decision makers, key donors, and donor prospects within the community. A video production may include video footage of your current programs and services; slides or photographs depicting your history; testimonials from program participants, active volunteers, or key donors; and a call to action or request for support from the viewers.

This vehicle can be used to communicate your mission, programs, and needs to corporate leaders or foundation directors who are difficult to meet in person. An ideal follow-up tool, it can be left with major gift prospects to perform additional "selling" in your absence. And, donors who live outside your region can also be made aware of new programs and opportunities. Other opportunities for presenting your videotape are information tables at meetings or conferences, or distribution to schools, churches, and civic groups that may have interest in supporting your cause.

While video productions can be very costly and beyond the budget of many small development programs, creativity and resourcefulness can often find an in-kind contributor to assist in this effort. The case example on page 112 shows how one organization developed its own "low cost" video.

In addition to professional video production studios, your organization may ask assistance from a local corporation with in-house video production capabilities, or you may use the studios available through your community access cable television station. Don't overlook the talent and skills of students at local community technical colleges who are often looking for projects to hone their skills. Also, be resourceful in obtaining donated videotapes from local businesses and/or free copying services for those multiple copies you will want to distribute.

Placemats or Tent Cards

Placemats or tent cards used at local schools, office cafeterias or fast-food restaurants provide an excellent opportunity to promote your organization's programs or events to a wide audience. Fast food restaurants often allow nonprofit groups to share the space on their placemats at no charge. For example, one of the most effective uses of this communication vehicle is the Ronald McDonald House program that is promoted throughout the country by McDonald's restaurants.

Tips for Trade Shows, Fairs and Special Events

The following marketing pieces can be distributed in a variety of venues, such as trade shows, county and state fairs, and sidewalk sales. They also may be given as donor gifts. Use them to increase the number of exposures to a mass audience. When used in conjunction with other media, they can help you boost your response by keeping your name around. If you have a campaign theme for your event or development program, don't forget to use your logo and slogan on your piece.

Mini rulers

Imprint lightweight plastic mini rulers with your organization's logo. You'd be surprised how often these easy-to-tuck-away rulers get used. They will help to increase the name recognition of your organization.

Bookmarks

Bookmarks are excellent stuffers for direct mail pieces and for distribution at trade fairs, libraries, and book stores. You can personalize these in many ways, depending on the audience you wish to reach. For example, if you are targeting health-conscious clients, you could include a fat or cholesterol counter. Try a bookmark for cooks, with common replacement measurements defined.

Try bookmarks of different shapes. How about a triangle fold that fits over the page corners of a book?

Stickers and Decals

Believe it or not, both children and adults just love stickers and decals. You can use large stickers for important phone numbers or print on slogans that are memorable. How about using a phone directory sticker for important safety numbers?

Refrigerator Magnets

Refrigerator magnets can provide daily reminders to your donors of your organization's name, mission, important programs and services, and/or phone number. It is an easy and economical way to maintain name awareness with your donor audience while providing them with a practical tool for the kitchen or office.

Small Card Enclosures

These economical cards can be used in a multitude of ways. Make them blank with your logo and phone number on the back, make them little thank-you cards. Be sure that the paper stock you use is heavy enough to fold without excessive bending and wrinkling. If you don't want to fold it, consider a triangle shape with a punch hole or die cut for attachment to a ribbon?

Puzzles or Games

Puzzles and games are great for the children you wish to influence. A coloring page puzzle, in well-defined, black-and-white contrast will intrigue many youngsters. You might also try a sheet of cards that can be cut apart to form a game. Fill-in-the-blank puzzles and connect-the-dots are perennial favorites. Put your creative mind to work in designing a game that fits with the mission of your

Case Example

By combining the organization's need for greater visibility with a video corporation's interest in supporting business and economics education, Junior Achievement of the Upper Midwest, Inc., was able to secure donated services to produce a multi-purpose videotape. This ten-minute video included testimonials from board members, volunteers, students, and teachers; footage of classroom programs; and historical and current program photographs. The video production firm expertly combined these visuals with voice-over and background music.

At the organization's annual benefit dinner/dance the tape had its debut. Many key volunteers and board members were very interested because they were able to see themselves "on stage."

The tape had many other uses. Additional copies were distributed to board members to promote the organization. It was also sent to key funders and prospects as part of a cultivation plan.

program. For example, an animal hunt might promote a zoo, or a puzzle of musical instruments could call attention to the civic orchestra?

Coloring Contest

A coloring contest is a perfect involvement device for children's programs. It's a good public relations trick to help children and parents remember your programs and services. No matter how many times it gets used, it still seems to create interest. Just make sure you have a nice prize or two for the winners!

Ornaments

Ornaments can commemorate a birthday, holiday, or some other special date. Try using these as donor cultivation tools, to remember the anniversary date of a donor's first gift.

Lists or Information Booklets

Easy-to-produce booklets and lists of "how to" tips or other pertinent information are perfect communication tools. Consider what purchases your clients or donors make, then create or compile information useful to them. If you are a health organization, for example, you could provide a list of low-cost suppliers for medicines. Use these booklets in your donor solicitation or prospecting program. Consider making them available to listeners or viewers who respond to your radio or television

presentations. For larger packages that require a membership contribution, you might add a newsletter, t-shirt, or some other premium.

Cross Promotions

Connecting your organization's mission and programs to a promotion for a commercial product or service effectively builds greater public awareness and revenues. However, a cross promotion can also damage your hard-earned reputation with the wrong type of partnership. Consider the problems that a chemical dependency organization might face if it accepted donations from a local brewery. Although this example may seem simplistic it is nonetheless highly important that you consider the ramifications of cross promotions before committing your organization.

Astute managers recognize that they must critically evaluate the consequences of promotional partnerships. Unfortunately, these consequences are not always easy to predict. Still, after serious consideration, you may feel that your risks are minimal and that you have much to be gained by such a partnership.

There are many different types of partnerships, some that require more long-term commitment. The following case example describes a bakery promotion that has proven itself as a successful partnership arrangement for all parties each year that it has been offered.

Small development shops can effectively let others raise funds for them by developing other effective "cause related marketing" opportunities. A portion of sales by customers at a department store, proceeds from coupons turned in by customers at grocery stores, revenue from special meals promoted by restaurants, a percentage of revenues generated by long distance telephone service providers, or even a dollar or two from each haircut at a barber shop are just a few ideas.

Be imaginative, persuasive, and persistent in seeking opportunities for cross promotions between your organization and community businesses. Remember, you'll extend your own capabilities if you use your key volunteers to help you approach businesses on your behalf.

Key Questions to Help You Plan Successful Events

Special events provide additional revenues, increased visibility, and an opportunity to involve more volunteers in your organization's mission. However, if events are not well planned and executed, they can drain the human and financial resources of a small development office.

Special fund raising events take many forms. Athletic events such as bike-a-

---

Case Example

In a successful partnership, a neighborhood bakery wishing to expand its clientele launched a marketing campaign with 25 local nonprofit agencies. The organization with the most votes received the opportunity to "staff" the bakery with its own volunteers and received a day's total sales.

The marketing for this event spanned a three-week period prior to the selection of the most popular nonprofit organization. The bakery placed an ad in the newspaper, asking customers to "vote" for their favorite candidate. Or, customers also had the option of going to the bakery to directly place their vote. Prior to the voting promotion, each of the 25 nonprofit organizations launched efforts to appeal to their constituencies for their "vote," through their newsletters, in special donor appeals, in public classes, or other existing marketing vehicles.

This format provided a mutual opportunity for the organizations and the bakery to increase revenues and public recognition.

thons, walk-a-thons, dance-a-thons, golf tournaments, 5K and 10K runs, and triathlons all provide opportunities for participants to support your organization through registration fees and pledged support of sponsors. Gala events such as charity balls, orchestra concerts, theater benefits, and tribute dinners allow your organization to generate revenue through ticket and table sales, live and silent auctions, raffles, and sponsorship opportunities.

Events may be closely aligned with an organization's mission such as a read-a-thon for libraries and literacy programs. Or, events may be designed to build a greater sense of community within schools, churches, or membership organizations promoting a particular cause. Special fund raising events also offer occasions to pay special recognition to key donors, members, volunteers, or community leaders through tribute dinners or celebrity roasts.

The key to success in conducting successful special fund raising events, as in all facets of fund raising, is to establish clear goals and objectives. Some questions that you may want to ask during the planning process are:

What do you want to accomplish with the event?

Is the goal of your event to increase visibility of your organization in the community, generate needed revenue, or a combination of both? You should first consider which internal and external audiences you wish to involve. How you promote the event will differ, depending on whether the event is targeted to children, adults, elderly, or families. Then, you should target your public relations efforts to these audiences by developing specific communication vehicles suited to their preferences. Communication devices may include TV, radio, newspapers, outdoor display ads, newsletters, written invitations, telephone calls, or personal meetings.

It is helpful to set a goal for the net profit that you want to realize from the event. Can the net results justify the cost in the eyes of the public? Will your event be designed to generate funds from current contributors, solicit the support of new donors, or receive support from both audiences? In determining the price of the event for each participant you should consider whether the price may serve as an attraction or possible deterrent to a larger audience. Different approaches may need to be planned to garner the support of distinct contributor or membership groups.

What investment is required, in terms of staff and volunteer time in order to successfully conduct the event?

Considering all your development responsibilities, do you, your staff, and volunteers have the time, talent, and resources necessary to conduct the event? During the planning stage

Your board and staff should determine if the projected net results will be worth the investment of human and financial resources.

it is necessary to determine how many staff and volunteers will have to be involved in the event in order to ensure its success. If your organization does not have sufficient human resources to conduct the event, you will need to identify additional sources of volunteer assistance. For example, an organization planning a 10K run may wish to enlist the help of volunteers from schools, churches, civic organizations, and the community-at-large to assist along the route of the run. Remember the Tom Sawyer approach to fund raising. Who can you enlist to share their time and talent in conducting your event? If your staff and volunteer core does not have the capability to successfully manage the event, you may wish to secure the assistance of a professional event planner to guide you.

Does your organization have the financial resources needed to sponsor the event?
Can your organization afford to host the event? In other words, if the event fails, can your organization afford to lose its financial investment? Before you begin a special event, prepare a budget that details expenses and projected income. After reviewing the budget, your board and staff should determine if the projected net results will be worth the investment of human and financial resources. If the budget indicates that revenues need to be increased, you

may wish to identify opportunities for individuals or corporate sponsors to underwrite the cost of the event. You may also want to investigate the possibility of a collaborative event with other nonprofit groups. By enlisting others as financial sponsors of your event you can lessen the financial exposure your organization may incur.

What is the timeline for the event?
Are you establishing a realistic timeline for your event or are you being pressured to conduct the event within a short time frame to meet the budgetary needs of your organization? A well-designed timeline is an essential ingredient for a successful event. Some events can be planned in a matter of weeks. Others may require a year or more of planning to ensure their success. Ongoing annual events, such as a gala ball, often require year-round planning.

In determining the timeline you should also consider the time of year that you wish to conduct the event. Are there any holidays or popular vacation periods that can detract attendance from the event? Also, consider what other community events might be competing for the attention and involvement of your donors, volunteers, and general public on the day of your event.

How will you use the event to cultivate volunteers, members, and donors?

Will your event provide current and new volunteers, members, and donors opportunities to become more invested in your organization by increasing their awareness of your mission, programs, and services? Educational components may offer your constituents the occasion to learn more about the work of your organization and the need for support. Your event could include a tour of your office or program facility, a photo display depicting your organization's history, a slide or video presentation highlighting your services, entertainment by program participants, or a testimonial from someone who has benefited from your services.

What will be the venue for the event?

As you plan for the event you should give careful consideration to the site at which the event will be held. If the event is to held outdoors, attention should be given to the season of the year and the possible effect of weather. A location that is safe, attractive, and accommodating to your audience will be a key factor in determining the success of your event. Consideration should also be given to handicap accessibility and parking.

What special needs will the event require?

How will you ensure compliance with all applicable laws and regulations? If your event is involved with gambling (raffles, bingo, casino games) or the sale or distribution of beer, wine, or liquor, you may be required to obtain a license or permit. Zoning regulations, crowd, or noise restrictions may also place limitations on your proposed event. You should also determine who will provide security, if required by your event.

How will you measure success and plan for the future?

An evaluation of the success of your event against the predetermined goals will help your organization plan for the future. By conducting a debriefing of staff and volunteers after the event you can evaluate the success and shortcomings of all aspects of the event. Further, if you plan to continue the event it will be important to assign leadership for the subsequent year.

Review Checklist

√ Has your organization developed strategies for promoting key messages to external publics ?

√ Has your organization identified its key publics and developed strategies appropriate to each segment?

√ Does your organization have a formalized structure in place for board recruitment, training, and cultivation?

√ Does your organization have a formalized structure in place for employee communications?

√ Has your organization a plan for crisis management in public relations? Does the system include ongoing, preventive activities as well as strategies and protocols for crisis situations?

√ Does your organization have a plan that clarifies who will be the organization's primary media contact? Does it specify how media relationships will be maintained?

√ Does your organization have a clear plan with goals and objectives for your special events?

√ Is your organization using a variety of cost-effective marketing communications, throughout the entire year?

Conclusion

Public relations is not an isolated event or celebration. It is an integral piece of the development program that reflects every aspect of your organization. An ongoing public relations program with your key publics will help your organization to maintain a positive image. It will also influence your revenues and ability to attract volunteers and in-kind services. Lastly, it will help your organization to recruit and retain capable staff.

If you do not have an effective public relations program in place, consider starting today. Any time you spend in developing such a plan will reward you again and again.

If you are already implementing public relations activities, take the time to evaluate their effectiveness. Consider new or additional options, if appropriate. You might discover new, more beneficial ways of boosting your results.

Major Gifts

- **Individual Gifts**
- **The Giving Pyramid**
- **Identifying Major Gift Donors**
- **Starting a Major Gifts Program**
- **Your Donor Family**
- **Major Gift Prospects Outside Your Organization**
- **Grants from Foundations**
- **Planned Giving**
- **Wills and Bequests Program**
- **Forms of Bequest**
- **Endowment Funds**

CHAPTER

6

Introduction

Writing grants, managing individual contributions, and conducting special events are the backbone of a strong development program. Yet, it is the cultivation of major gifts that will provide a solid base of support for present and future organizational efforts.

Every organization defines major gifts in different ways. The definition often depends upon the highest gift amount that your donors are capable of giving. For some organizations, $100 is a major gift. Others set the standard at $500, $1,000, or $10,000. No matter what the size of your organization's major gifts, you should be cultivating each donor to higher giving levels through a major gift program.

Individual Gifts

The Giving Pyramid

Nearly ninety percent of all charitable gifts originate from individuals. Twenty percent of the total number of these gifts will normally provide eighty percent or more of the total revenue for an organization. For some organizations, as few as five percent of the number of gifts will provide most of the revenue dollars. Observe the giving pyramid, Illustration 18. It shows why the gifts of just a few donors make such a significant differ- ence and why it is so vital to cultivate major gifts.

This giving pyramid is the trade standard for calculating the number of gifts and the various giving amounts needed for campaigns. Because it is so consistent, it can be used as one method of evaluating your own development program. How many donors are at the top of your program's individual giving pyramid? If you have only one to two percent at the top, with little or no increase in gift amounts from the bottom section to the top, then you may wish to spend more time in cultivating up-graded or increased gifts from individuals. An organization with few or no major gifts will spend more money to raise a dollar than an organization whose donor giving patterns follow the ideal pyramid structure.

Some fund raisers believe that the way to cultivate major gifts is to find wealthy individuals. Rather, you will find it easier to consider your "friends" as major gift prospects and hope that some of them are wealthy. Major gifts most frequently originate from your existing file of donors.

You may be saying to yourself, "But I know that none of my donors are capable of giving major gifts." Others have said the same thing. They also have also discovered that thoughtful planning, concerted effort, and an investment of time helped to hasten the arrival of major gifts.

How to Identify Major Gift Donors For Your Organization

How can a staff member or volunteer working in a small development office handle myriad tasks and still find time to develop relationships with major individual donors?

First of all, you and your organization must be committed to major gift fund raising. In order to be successful, a significant share of your development resources, including staff, time, and budget, will need to be allocated to major gift cultivation.

Secondly, you must focus your work on a manageable number of "core" donors who are the most generous contributors or who offer the greatest potential for substantial gifts. For example, from the top 100 donors who contribute to your organization, you might pick the top 5, 10, or 20, to cultivate as "core" donors. A tool to help you in the selection process is Illustration 4: Prospect Rating Form, in Chapter 2, page 21.

Major gift donors are identified by three key indicators:

■ Recency since the last donation,

■ Frequency of gifts within a certain time frame, and

■ Amount of the gifts being given.

Illustration 18: Giving Pyramid

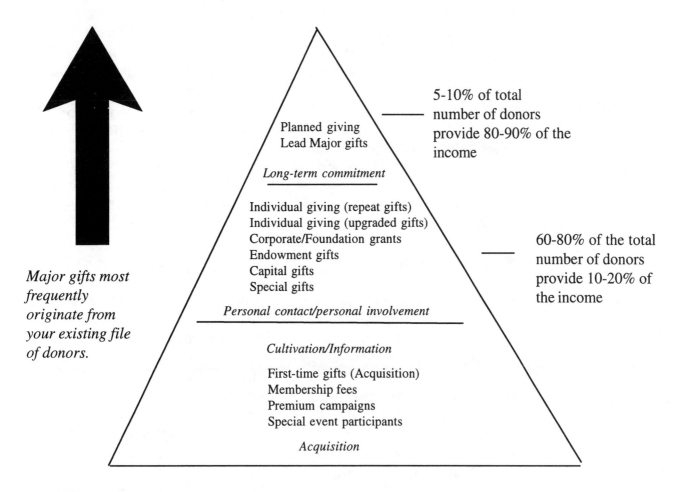

5-10% of total number of donors provide 80-90% of the income

Planned giving
Lead Major gifts

Long-term commitment

Individual giving (repeat gifts)
Individual giving (upgraded gifts)
Corporate/Foundation grants
Endowment gifts
Capital gifts
Special gifts

Personal contact/personal involvement

60-80% of the total number of donors provide 10-20% of the income

Cultivation/Information

First-time gifts (Acquisition)
Membership fees
Premium campaigns
Special event participants

Acquisition

Major gifts most frequently originate from your existing file of donors.

The goal: moving donors up to higher levels

Each of these indicators is a key measurement of donor and member interest and commitment. Careful analysis of your database records, based on these indicators, will help you to identify your core group of donors and members.

Other factors or activities that indicate interest in your organization are:

■ Attendance at open houses and special activities;

■ Volunteer involvement;

■ Participation on the board of directors or board committees;

■ Longevity as a donor or member;

■ Contributions to capital or endowment campaigns;

■ Involvement with development and marketing campaigns;

■ Contributions to other organizations in your community.

A single instance of participation is less an indicator than a history of repeated involvement.

Starting a Major Gifts Program

We have already mentioned the need to commit time and resources to a major gift program to ensure its success. How can you accomplish this? One option is to recruit as major gifts officer, one board member, volunteer, or staff member who has longevity and commitment to the organization. Then, assign that person five to eight prospects from among your core donor group.

The volunteer major gifts officer will become the key contact between you, your staff, and the donor. The volunteer will continue to develop a deeper relationship with the donor for the next year or more. He or she will maintain personal contact, informing the major donor prospect about critical events affecting the organization. As well, the volunteer major gift officer will determine the donor's needs and will work with you in developing opportunities for the donor to participate in the organization, financially and personally.

You, of course will need to manage the volunteer or staff member by providing support at critical times. Nonetheless, this major gifts officer will save you, the development manager, a considerable amount of time.

The following list provides just a sample of some activities for your major gift cultivation program:

■ A complete communication plan, including newsletters, annual reports and personalized solicitation letters that request new, repeat or increased giving;

■ Invitation to special programs and receptions; recruitment for advisory board, leadership, or other important volunteer positions;

■ Invitations to personally meet with your organization's executive director or chair of the board;

■ Special phone calls and letters thanking them for their gifts;

■ Public recognition for their gifts in publications and on donor walls;

■ Inclusion in donor giving clubs;

■ Invitation to make special gifts, planned gifts or capital campaign gifts;

■ Roles on the board of directors or as fund raising campaign chairs;

■ Opportunities to assist in identifying other major donor gift prospects.

How to Cultivate Major Donors

The discussion of segmentation strategies earlier in this book explained the need to treat your donor or members differently, depending upon their involvement with your organization.

Consider the following analogy in relationship to major gift donors. How do you relate to members of your family compared to your co-workers or acquaintances in the community? Naturally, you are much more likely to invest greater time and effort in relationships with immediate family members and others who are important to you. Similarly, you will want to treat your major donors as members of the organization's family. Remember their birthdays and anniversaries, and seek opportunities to include them in your organizational celebrations and activities.

Your relationships with major donors will be developed over a long period of time. With each passing year, you will become more aware of the donors' needs, concerns, and accomplishments. In order to fully respond to their interests, you must be prepared to communicate frequently.

Meet with major gift donors for lunch or a home visit. By practicing good listening skills, you can help major donors identify their specific interests and help them achieve their own personal mission through their philanthropic activities. Donors, in turn, will help your organization to meet its goals.

It is important to develop an individualized plan for each major donor. It is equally important to allow major donors the opportunity to set the pace of this relationship with your organization. You can assist them by giving them freedom of choice as to what programs, services, or special projects they wish to support. Similarly, you will honor their choices as to the size of gift they wish to donate, the type of giving vehicles they want to use, and even the frequency and type of communications they wish to receive.

Including Other Members of Your Donor's Family

Because major gifts often represent significant contributions by a family or business, it is very important to include the key decision makers in the presentation and solicitation. Thus, you must seek to nurture the relationship with all contributors within the family so that there is a strong sense of ownership. This will serve your organization well if something should occur that would interfere with the relationship, such as a death in the family. In the event that one spouse passes away, the commitment and involvement of the surviving spouse will remain with your organization.

How to Identify Major Gift Prospects Outside Your Organization

Donor prospect research, as described in Chapter 2, is key to your ability to identify donor prospects who have the means, interest, and propensity to give major gifts. These cost effective

It is important to develop an individualized plan for each major donor. It is equally important to allow major donors the opportunity to set the pace of this relationship with your organization.

techniques will assist you greatly in your major gifts search. Use the techniques that are most appropriate for your situation.

Perhaps a more important resource available to you are your current major gift donors. Your major donors may be willing to identify prospects or open doors to other prospects through letters, phone calls, or personal introductions. By getting your donors involved in developing the relationship with new prospects from the start, you may also encourage them to continue to assist you in the ongoing research, rating, cultivation, solicitation, and recognition efforts.

Planned Giving

A planned giving program provides an opportunity for donors to achieve significant goals in their philanthropy while strengthening the long term financial stability of your organization. Donors can do this in creative ways, utilizing their assets such as securities, real estate, insurance and personal property, in addition to cash. Planned gift arrangements can provide donors with significant savings on income, gift, and estate taxes and enable donors to preserve income during their lifetime.

Experts estimate that more than half of all charitable gifts will be made through planned giving arrangements by the turn of the century. For this reason, planned giving must be included in the development efforts of all organizations.

Small development shops may shy away from planned giving programs because they seem too technical, involve too much time, use financial resources that are needed to meet the current budget, and often require several years of investment before financial returns can be realized. Yet, in the long run, planned giving can prove to be the most cost effective form of fund raising.

Planned giving may take any of these forms:

- A will or bequest
- Life insurance
- Cash
- Stock
- Trust or annuities

Many development managers believe that they do not have the capacity within their donor base to secure major planned gifts. However, organizations throughout the country are continually surprised by the receipt of large estate gifts from donors who appeared to be cash poor while they were alive. These same donors who could only afford to contribute small annual gifts may have owned property or investments of considerable value that they designated as planned gifts upon their death.

The best candidates for planned gifts are individuals aged 55+, without heirs. Notice that there is no mention of income. In fact, many planned gifts originate from those with only modest incomes. Still, individuals with wealth are also planned giving candidates. The one characteristic that all planned giving donors share is a serious commitment to the organization.

Planned Giving Basics

Bequests

Bequests offer the simplest, most flexible, planned gift. Bequests are made in wills, living trusts, and other estate plans. Types of bequests include:

- Specific Outright Bequest which designates a fixed amount or specific property.

- Residuary or Remainder Bequest which allows the donor to designate a percent or portion of the estate to charity after other distributions have been made.

- Contingent Bequest which designates a gift to charity only if certain circumstances are met.

Life Income Gifts

Life Income Gifts offer the donor income in return for making an

In the long run, planned giving can prove to be the most cost effective form of fund raising.

125

irrevocable gift to charity. The income may be variable or fixed and last for lifetime(s), a certain number of years, or both. They include:

- Gift annuities that provide the donor with a contractual promise of fixed income in return for a charitable gift.

- A charitable remainder trust provides income to the donor's beneficiaries and the remainder to charity.

The preparation and adoption of clear and thorough policies and guidelines for planned giving are essential steps for success.

Other Planned Gifts

- A life estate provides a charity with the gift of a residence or farm while allowing the donor the right to continue to live there for the remainder of his or her life.

- A charitable lead trust provides a charity with income for a term of years and leaves the remainder to the donor's heirs.

- Life insurance designations allow a charity to receive benefits upon the death of the insured.

Planned Giving for the One-Person Shop

Your small development office can realize great success in the area of planned giving, but only if you in-

clude other staff and volunteers in the effort.

One of the best ways to implement a planned giving program is through a planned giving advisory committee. The committee is formed with the purpose of providing you, the development manager, with program ideas, technical knowledge, connections to the community, and credibility for your planned giving program.

Financial planners, attorneys, bank trust officers, accountants, real estate brokers, insurance agents, stock brokers, marketing specialists, key donors, and long-term volunteers are essential players on the planned giving advisory committee. These individuals will provide you with expertise in developing policies and procedures, preparing marketing plans, identifying prospects, promoting the program, meeting with prospects, soliciting gifts, and acknowledging donors.

The preparation and adoption of clear and thorough policies and guidelines for planned giving are essential steps for success. Since many gift vehicles guarantee specific rates of return, it is imperative that your organization be prepared to steward such gifts in a way that will benefit your donors and your organization. Policy statements and written procedures will guide you in accepting and managing gifts of life insurance, appreciated securities, or real estate.

It is important to know before the gift is offered, how you and your organization intend to respond to proposed planned gifts. For instance, can your organization assure the donor a specific fixed percentage return on a charitable trust or annuity? Should your organization accept a gift of real estate without first conducting an environmental audit to determine any environmental hazards that may exist on the property? How will you account for the value of a gift that your organization may not actually receive for many years? To protect the interests of your organization and fulfill the wishes of the donor, it is extremely important to have written policies to serve as your guide.

Small organizations with limited financial management capabilities may wish to consider using the investment and marketing services of a community foundation. Community foundations throughout the country are enabling small nonprofit organizations to develop and manage strong planned giving programs through the professional capabilities and assistance of the foundation staff.

Starting Simple with a Wills and Bequests Program

If you are new to planned giving, the body of knowledge that encompasses the field can seem overwhelming. Ever-changing laws, regulations, IRS rulings, marketing strategies, gift vehicles, ethical considerations, and donors' motivations can frighten even seasoned development professionals away from this extremely important source of revenue.

Although it is important to become knowledgeable in this area, you can begin today with a simple wills and bequests program, where the donor includes your organization as a beneficiary.

You can promote a simple wills program in your newsletter, annual report, special mailings and in your personal meetings with donors and prospects. One could assume that most people already have made up their minds about their wills and to whom they intend to leave their assets upon death. However, approximately only one out of ten people in this country have a will and even those who do may continue to make changes in their designated beneficiaries throughout their lives.

A wills program can be promoted by highlighting the impact a gift received through a donor's bequest had on your organization. Or, if your organization has yet to receive an estate gift

Small organizations with limited financial management capabilities may wish to consider using the investment and marketing services of a community foundation.

127

in this manner, you may choose to feature donors in your newsletter or annual report who explain why it has been important to them to include your organization in their will and what they hope their gift will accomplish for your organization and the people it serves.

Who should lead the way in starting a wills and bequests program? Your board, key volunteers, major donors, executive staff, and you, yourself, should take the lead and set the example for others by designating your organization in a will. The amount of the gift or percentage of the estate that donors designate in their wills does not have to be public knowledge. However, because they have indicated this commitment to your organization it may serve to motivate others to give in a like manner.

One of the best ways to promote a wills and bequests program is to provide sample language that may be used in designating your charity through a will. Language similar to that used in the following examples can be adopted by your organization in marketing its planned giving program. To avoid possible legal implications, the organization should never imply that they are providing legal advice. Even though examples are provided, the organization should remind individuals to seek legal advice.

Forms of Bequest

The following are samples of wording that may be used in preparing different forms of bequests through a will. The authors strongly suggest that all individuals consult a legal advisor when making a will or bequest.

Specific Outright Bequest

This is the most common type of bequest clause, giving away a specific amount of money, a specific piece of property, or both.

Example
" I give, devise and bequeath to [name of organization], a [name of state] nonprofit corporation, located at [city and state], [summary/description of property] to be used for its

_____ purposes. I further direct that interest or other income which may be earned by said bequest shall also be paid to [name of organization] from the date of my decease until paid."

Residuary or Remainder Bequest

This type of bequest gives a specified portion of assets remaining in the estate after all debts, taxes, expenses, and other bequests have been paid.

Example
"I give, devise and bequeath to [name of organization], [name of state] nonprofit corporation, located at [city and

state], the rest [or percentage] of the property of my estate to be used for its _____ purposes. I further direct that interest or other income which may be earned by said bequest shall also be paid to [name of organization] from the date of my decease until paid."

Contingent Bequest

This bequest takes effect if something unexpected occurs. It ensures that an organization receives the bequest instead of an unintended beneficiary.

Example
"In the event that _____ shall not survive me, or shall die within ninety days of the date of my death, or as the result of a common disaster, then I give, devise and bequeath said sum (property) to [name of organization], a [name of state] nonprofit corporation, located at [city and state], to be used for its _____ purposes. I further direct that interest or other income which may be earned by said bequest shall also be paid to [name of organization] from the date of my decease until paid. "

Start today with a simple planned giving program. As you begin to achieve success, you may decide that you need additional support from an outside consultant. Before launching a more comprehensive planned giving program you will want to

ensure that your board is committed to the project and that many have made their own planned gift as demonstration of this approval. Equally important is that sufficient financial resources are available for implementation of the planned giving program.

Endowment Fund

An endowment fund can provide the foundation for the future financial security of your organization. The endowment is like a savings account where the principal of the fund remains intact, using earned interest earned to support the organization's programs, services, and capital needs. Donors who wish to leave a legacy gift to your organization may feel that an endowment fund is attractive because it will allow their gifts to support your mission in perpetuity.

Because donors who give to endowment most often give from their net assets rather than cash flow, their gifts are more likely to be the largest gift they ever make to your organization, often surpassing their lifetime cumulative giving.

An endowment fund can provide the foundation for the future financial security of your organization.

Donors who make a current gift or pledge a contribution to an endowment fund often prove to be very loyal and generous contributors to the annual operating needs of the organization. Their current and future gifts do not become an either/or proposition. Rather, these gifts should serve to enhance each other. Making this clear in your communications with the donor is essential in order to ensure that you continue to receive a variety of different types of gifts from these special donors

Even the small development shop may benefit from the creation of an endowment fund. If your organization has not established an endowment fund, you may wish to encourage your board to do so. This will provide you with an especially attractive marketing tool to be used in your major gifts and planned giving programs. Your organization may choose to manage the fund or you may rely on the expertise of outside resources such as community foundations.

By providing this service to your donors, whereby they receive professional guidance on making tax-wise and donor-beneficial gifts, you will ensure the economic future of your organization and increase contributions from your loyal supporters.

Good proposals are never conceived without careful planning and knowledge of the external environment that affects your organization's programs and services.

Grants from Foundations

As the funding environment becomes more and more competitive, excellent communication skills and well-documented, results-oriented proposals will be the requirements for success. We hope that this chapter has explained the need to fine-tune your communications with all types

of donors. This is also true of communications with foundations. Although proposals may differ slightly in terms of funder requirements, all proposals should be developed according to the conceptual framework described below.

Grant Research

Good proposals are never conceived without careful planning and knowledge of the external environment that affects your organization's programs and services. In other words, what other service providers or vendors, if any, are doing the work or providing the product that you propose? Will you use this grant to capitalize on existing knowledge, build the knowledge base, or develop new ideas? New ideas are always welcomed by funders, but they also are interested in projects that are cost-effective and that have proven results.

Call a foundation staff member to discuss the project. You may wish to "test" a few ideas to see how well they are received. Of course, once you find that there might be a positive fit, you will need to secure the foundations guidelines, if any are available.

In addition, when developing a proposal, you may wish to make sure that you have considered the concepts suggested in the chapters on Public Relations and Planning. Foundations are always more receptive to proposals that show a strong planning component utilizing key members of the target population, other service agencies, or key leaders in the field.

Here are the major sections typically included in a grant proposal:

Executive Summary

The executive summary reiterates the key points within your proposal. When space is available, the lead-in summary provides an overall picture to give the reader a base for understanding. If useful, it may provide a historical perspective about the organization. The length of the summary is usually ten percent of the total proposal. Depending on how the executive summary is structured, you may also wish to add additional paragraphs describing your target population and target geographic area to be served.

Problem Statement

Short and compelling, the problem statement appears before the needs assessment explanation. If possible, it quantifies the problem, along with an explanation. One example might be: *An estimated 20 percent of the total number of persons, age 55 and above, do not have adequate health care. This problem contributes an estimated $1,000,000 to the cost of public supported health care that* *could be minimized by adequate prevention activities.*

The paragraphs following would document this statement, through statistical evidence, anecdotal information, or statements from authorities. This is called the needs assessment. The needs assessment often is a good place to describe the competitive position of the organization within the overall service delivery system. In other words, why is your particular organization the best one to provide the proposed services or proposed product? This is an essential question to answer, particularly if there are other organizations that provide similar services.

Grant Project Activities or Method

This section describes your solution to the problem statement, in terms of measurable goals and objectives. A time line may be included in this section, or in a separate chart, depending on the space allowed by the funder. You may have only one or two goals, with several objectives, depending on your overall vision. Or, you may wish to state your objectives in terms of percentages, rather than numbers. The important concept is to quantify the work you will actually perform. A detailed description is necessary. For example, following the problem statement above, you might state:

Goal: To improve preventive health care for persons age 55 and above.

Objective: To provide free annual check-ups, with regular blood pressure monitoring, cancer screening tests, and EKG testing. A total of 200 individuals will be served. 80% of client database (of approximately 200) will participate in regular preventive health care screening tests.

Capability

This section describes the qualifications and accomplishments of the organization and its key personnel. It may include documentation of accreditation and testimonials from experts in the field or the organization's clients.

Evaluation

Directly related to your goals and objectives, this section describes how you will evaluate your progress. This may include focus groups, written surveys, or actual changes in the incidence of the problem that can be documented by local records. It should also include who will complete the evaluation and how the results will be used.

Persistence Pays Off

Because of the increased competitive climate in grant seeking, fewer funders are willing to make grants to new organizations. Operating funds are also becoming more scarce. Don't despair! Despite these adverse conditions, many organizations continue to increase their yearly grant revenues and/or number of new gifts every year.

If you are declined for a grant, you may wish to call the funder to discover the reasons why. If it appears that it was a project they felt had some merit, you may wish to try again in the following grant cycle. It is not uncommon for a first-time major grant request ($50,000 and above) to have to be submitted for a second or third time. Evaluate your proposal in terms of any weaknesses the foundation officer might identify. In subsequent submissions your diligence will pay off!

Review Checklist

√   At what giving level does your organization designate a gift to be a major gift?

√   Does the largest segment of your private sector contributions come from a few key donors?

√   Who are your organization's core donors?

√ What special cultivation strategies do you have in place for your major donors?

√ Is your organization committed to planned giving and endowment development? Has the board approved the project? Has the board made a commitment in terms of their own gifts?

√ Have you formed a Planned Giving Advisory Committee?

√ Does your organization have clear and current policies and procedures for planned giving and endowment?

√ Is the problem statement of your proposal succinct and easy to understand?

√ Is the needs assessment section of your grant proposal well documented with research and quantified in numbers, if appropriate?

√ Is the methods section of your proposal easy for a lay person to understand? Is it free of jargon? Does the method provide a solution to the problem statement?

√ Does the methods section of your proposal have measurable goals and objectives? Are they reasonable? If results are obtained, will the project be worthwhile?

√ Does the evaluation section relate to the method and problem? Is the best method being used to evaluate outcomes, considering cost-efficiencies?

√ Does the capability section of your proposal explain organizational capabilities as related to the proposed work ?

Conclusion

Paying special attention to your major donors is essential for a successful development program. Individualized cultivation plans, communications, solicitations, and recognition are important ingredients of major gifts programs. Involving major donors in planned giving programs not only helps them in meeting their own personal goals in life and often benefiting their heirs, but will help build a strong financial foundation for your organization's future.

Donor Solicitation and Communications

CHAPTER

7

■ *Make it Easy for Your Donors to Give*

■ *Evaluating Promotional Results*

■ *Is Direct Mail Appropriate for Your Organization?*

■ *Everything You Ever Wanted to Know about Lists*

■ *Technology for Marketing Management*

■ *Profitable Marketing and Fund Raising Ideas*

■ *New Ideas from the Field*

Introduction

In the United States today there are more than one million nonprofit organizations all vying for the same donor dollar. Such intense competition requires that organizations use innovative methods to grab the attention of donors and donor prospects, get them involved in some way with their organization, and finally persuade them to contribute.

To raise funds successfully in a small development shop you must be creative in your approaches to donors. You need to offer them a variety of ways in which to support your organization and make it easy for them to give. Many development directors are already using the following methods to seek donor gifts. You may wish to evaluate the number and type of gift giving opportunities which your organization makes available to its donors. This chapter highlights many ways in which to solicit gifts from your donors.

Make It Easy for Your Donors to Give

Several options can bring additional dollars into your organization. Some of them are surprisingly simple, while others may require an initial investment. Even though this investment may be required, many of these options should be seriously considered. In the long term, the payback could be substantial.

Credit Cards

Those plastic cards that we have come to rely on in our day-to-day shopping and purchase of services can also be one of the most effective vehicles for securing donor contributions.

Credit card options for donor giving should be an essential part of all development programs. Charitable contributions given through credit

Case Example

The Children's Home Society of Minnesota has a tradition-rich annual holiday direct mail campaign called Little Red Stocking. Inspired by the concept of this campaign, volunteers embraced the idea of giving actual little red stockings to the children served by the agency. Children ranging in age from infants to ten years.

A promotion was developed to brighten the holidays of these children in need. Volunteers believed it would also offer excitement, fun, and many rewards for the Society's volunteers. The concept is simple. Donors sponsor little red stockings for $25 each and the society sends stockings to the children. Stuffed inside the stockings are hand-knit hats, mittens, scarves and age-appropriate toys. The donors receive the child's artwork, which thanks them for the gift.

Although planning is a yearlong process, the development manager spends only 10 percent of her time managing the promotion. Almost entirely volunteer-driven, the Little Red Stocking promotion seeks volunteers from businesses, senior centers, and churches throughout the Minneapolis-St. Paul area. A volunteer committee provides leadership for the effort.

Initially, volunteers were recruited individually. But now, many work together as groups, staffing an entire day of activities. Many parent volunteers enjoy the opportunity to work together with their children during the three-day stocking stuffing event.

Local activity centers and senior housing centers are contacted to recruit knitters to make the hats, mittens and scarves. In 1996, 500 volunteers staffed this entire event, including a 97-year-old knitter. Her enthusiasm lent credibility to the idea that one is never too old to be a valuable volunteer.

The beauty of the promotion is its simplicity. A local ration station sponsors the vent, proving airtime until the fund raising goal is reached. This includes live interviews with staff and volunteers, including human interest stories straight from the agency's files.

Because donors call the agency themselves, the phone volunteer does no solicitation. He or she fills out a pledge card which indicates the donor's wishes. This eliminates the need for lengthy training. The volunteers simply sends the payment invoice, envelopes and child's artwork to the new sponsor. The agency then sends three follow-up reminders to ensure that pledges are fulfilled. The fulfillment rate on pledges is an astounding 98 percent!

The promotion increases its revenues each year. In 1988, its first year, the sponsorship of 950 stocking raised $23,750. In 1996, sponsors were obtained for 1,600 stockings, with $40,000 in gross income. A working budget, equivalent to 25 percent of the expected gross proceeds, is used to purchase yarn and toys at wholesale prices and to pay for the printing of pledge cards and campaign materials. Donations are also secured.

The net proceeds for 1996 was $30,000--an excellent return for a promotion that rewards volunteers, brightens the holidays for many children, and is so much fun that it hardly seems like work.

Little Red Stocking Campaign

DATE: _____   TIME: _____

Children's Home Society
OF MINNESOTA

Administrative Offices
1605 Eustis Street
St. Paul, Minnesota 55108

AMOUNT DUE
$ _____
PAYMENT METHOD
❑ Check enclosed.
❑ Charge (VISA or MasterCard)
Credit card # _____
Expiration date _____
Signature _____

_____

_____

_____

PHONE: _____

Thank You

PLEASE PAY FROM THIS INVOICE — THANK YOU
WHITE—Customer Copy   YELLOW—Return with Payment   PINK—File Copy

Illustration 19-2; Children's Home Society Radio Program Solicitation Card

Front of card, in red, green, and black

Donor card, with child's drawing on inside.
Personalized, using name of donor, included name and age of sponsored child

Illustration 19-3; Children's Home Society Little Red Stocking Promotion Letter

November 1996

Dear Friend of Children,

"No, Mama; no, Mama!"

From his crib, Danny cried out his first plea for help, not for his mother's protection, but to be protected from his mother.

Danny started life healthy, chubby, bright-eyed and full of hope. He deserved to be nurtured and loved. However, Danny's early years were rough ones.

It is hurtful for all of us to hear that such a precious little baby was ignored, burned, slapped, hit and left in his crib alone for endless hours at a time. The sparkle, which was once in Danny's eyes, was soon replace by tears and despair. He lived his early childhood between home and foster families while efforts were made to help his mom become a better parent.

At age four, Danny was placed in long-term county foster care. While foster homes provide children with much needed care, the goal is that these children be placed in permanent, adoptive homes. They need parents who will love and protect them, be role models for them and, most of all, provide a family and home they can always call their own.

Children's Home Society's Special Needs Adoption Program actively recruits and prepares families to adopt these children. It also provides ongoing counseling and support to children and their adoptive parents.

Through the efforts of Children's Home Society, Danny was placed in an adoptive family at the age of six. Now, two years later, Danny is eager to learn, starting on his Little League team, beginning to trust and respect adults, and feeling proud of himself. The sparkle in his eyes is back.

(over, please)

Children's Home Society, Administrative Offices, 1605 Eustis St., St. Paul, MN 55108 • 612/646-7771

Illustration 19-4; Children's Home Society direct mail reply device, front and reverse

Gift "ask" keyed to donor's last gift

Little Red Stocking

Help shape a lifetime...
Your gift will make a difference!

Enclosed is my gift of:
_____ $50.00 _____ $100.00 _____ $150.00 _____ Other $ _____
Or please charge my gift of $ _____ to my
VISA/MasterCard# _____ Expires _____
Signature _____

I96   ab

Diane Hodiak
43 West Hampton
Minneapolis, MN 55423

IıldıılıdılıdııılllıııldıldıdıılllllıııIlıdılıldıl

Please make checks payable to the Children's Home Society.
Children's Home Society of Minnesota is eligible to receive tax-deductible gifts.

WO09

*Thanks for helping make
this holiday season special.*

The Puckett Family.

Children's Home Society of Minnesota is a
nonprofit, federally registered 501(c)(3)
organization. Copies of our annual report
or financial statements are available by
contacting Development and Community
Relations at the address below.

An independent source of information about
Children's Home Society of Minnesota or any
other charity is your state attorney general's
office. In Minnesota, you may also check with
the Charities Review Council.

Children's Home Society
Administrative Offices
1605 Eustis Street
St. Paul, Minnesota 55108
612/646-7771

*Children's Home Society of Minnesota, with your help
and support, is able to improve the lives of children.*

OUR PROGRAMS _____

Child Care Services
Nineteen centers throughout Minnesota
School-Age Day Care Shelter

Adoption Services
Open Adoption/Pregnancy Counseling
International Adoption
American Infant Adoption
Special Needs Adoption
Post Adoption Services

Child Abuse Prevention Services
Five Crisis Nursery sites
Family Mentor Program
Parent Education and Support

Children's Home Society
OF MINNESOTA
Leadership and excellence
in child care, adoption and
child abuse prevention.
1889

Reverse side, direct mail solicitation reply device

Illustration 19-5, Children's Home Society Exterior and Return Envelope

Return envelope, radio program pledge

Effective use of celebrity teaser copy

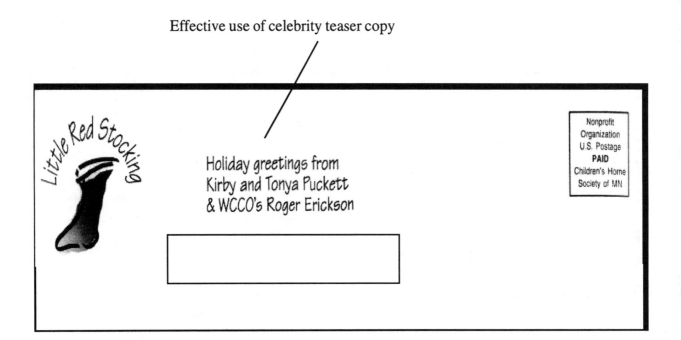

Direct mail exterior envelope, window type

charges allow organizations the opportunity to secure gifts through the mail, over the telephone, or in person. Credit card options should be offered on all reply return devices in direct mail packages. Credit cards also facilitate increased purchase of tickets for special events and auctions. In sum, credit cards facilitate giving and encourage many donors to make a larger gift than they might be able to make by check or cash.

Banks will charge a small service fee for handling these gift transactions but organizations often will recoup the difference in these costs by assuring that gift pledges are received and often at a higher fulfillment level than by other means. In a small development shop, credit card giving is an easy means to secure gifts.

Electronic Fund Transfer

Another giving vehicle that can easily be established by a small development shop is an electronic fund transfer (EFT) program for donors. This program, which can be set up by your bank, allows donors to make a monthly, quarterly, or annual pledge to your organization and have the contribution electronically transferred from their bank account to your organization's account on a regular basis. You may need to have a minimum number of donors before this system becomes cost-effective. Nonetheless, you should explore EFT as an

option for your development program.

This type of program makes it very easy for your donors to give and also assures 100 percent fulfillment on pledges. The pledge remains in effect until the donor upgrades the amount or cancels the pledge. This is perhaps the most effective way to assure that donor pledges will continue to be received.

If an organization decides that an EFT program is not appropriate at the current time, then it can also implement another method to encourage pledge collection. Send the donor a set or booklet of coupons, with envelopes, each with a due date. This will save your organization money because you will eliminate the need to repeatedly generate pledge reminders Still, it is a good idea to follow-up with these pledge coupon programs, to make sure that your donors are using them.

Payroll Deduction

United Way programs throughout the country long ago proved the benefit of establishing payroll deduction programs for charitable giving. It is a simple and relatively painless way for donors to support their favorite charities on a monthly or annual basis.

The donor's pledge payments are deducted from the donor's paycheck,

Case Example

One human service organization has enlisted more than 100 donors in a monthly gift program through electronic fund transfer. This program assures the organization of committed donors and continued cash flow. The organization's bank sends it a statement each month showing the names and amounts of contributions.

(Sample Authorization Card)

AUTHORIZATION FOR AUTOMATIC PAYMENT

I authorize ABC Organization and the bank named below to charge my account each / / month / / quarter in accordance with the conditions on the reverse side of this form.

Monthly/Quarterly Amount $ _____

Donor's Signature _____ Date _____

Your name (Please print) _____

Your Address (Street, City, Zip) _____

Name of your bank: _____

Address of your bank: _____

Checking Account Number: _____

PLEASE RETURN TOP HALF TO ABC ORGANIZATION

RETAIN FOR YOUR RECORDS
On _____ I authorized _____
    (Date)   (Name of your bank)

for the amount of $_____ each / / month / / quarter to initiate electronic entries to my checking account and agreed to the terms listed on the authorization.

I understand that my account will be charged on the 15th of each month or quarter.

This authorization to charge my account shall be the same as if I personally signed a check to ABC Organization. The record of my payment will be included in my bank statement.

The authority I give to charge my account will remain in effect until I notify ABC Organization in writing to terminate the authorization. All information is strictly confidential.

accumulated with the contributions of others within the company or organization, and then sent in one check to the charity on a regular basis. This system is ideal because contributions are deducted from the pay check before donors are paid, thus not requiring them to make choices between other financial commitments. The gift payment will continue until terminated by the donor.

In addition to United Way programs, many alternative workplace giving programs have been established throughout the country to support the arts, environmental groups, medical organizations, international relief agencies, and other community services. Investigate federated funds you might join, and benefit from their workplace campaigns in your community.

Some organizations have established their own payroll deduction programs within companies and organizations that are owned by board members, committed donors, corporations, and businesses. While this may prove to be a very labor intensive program to establish, small development shops can enlist the support of employees, business leaders, and volunteers to assist in this effort. Don't forget to establish a payroll deduction program for employees within your own organization.

Donor Envelopes

In every promotion, making donor envelopes available will improve your results. In the preceding case study of the Children's Home Society, the extraordinary pledge fulfillment rate could be attributed to the three reminder envelopes that were sent out to donors to secure their pledges.

At the same time, however, it is equally important that you continue to evaluate which situations are most profitable for including a return envelope. Compare dollars raised and response rates with the costs of production and associated postage costs, if any. You may find, for example, that current donors will respond equally favorably to a non-postage paid envelope as they will to a postage-paid envelope.

Try a variety of methods to make it easy for your donors to make contributions to your organization. Make envelopes available in your office reception area; distribute them at special events and speaking engagements; insert them into newsletters and annual reports; and include them with thank-you letters to donors. Although some organizations find the latter to seem inappropriate, successful development programs have learned that the "bounce back" effect of envelopes being supplied with donor acknowledgments is a very effective and low-cost means of generating additional income.

An investment in donor envelopes is one which will surely pay for itself in a short time. A development shop with limited resources may find that the donation and printing of envelopes can be one way in which a business or corporation may be willing to assist your organization at a time when they do not have the financial resources to make a monetary gift.

Evaluating Promotional Results

Additional valuable information about how to evaluate your fund raising programs can be found in Chapter 2, *Research*. Included here are some specific methods to use in evaluating marketing communications. For example, if you are having a hard time distinguishing where, or which campaigns your envelopes are coming from, consider the following suggestions:

Printed Key Codes

An efficient method of tracking the success of your mail campaigns is to print key codes on the return envelope to indicate the type of campaign and/ or mail date. For instance, a holiday mailing in November 1996 could be coded HN96. Even if a donor were to use the return envelope many months or years later, your organization could track the source of the gift as well as the instrumental campaign.

Printing a code on envelopes can be done at no extra charge at the time the envelope is printed. However, if you are printing envelopes for several different campaigns or printing the codes on the envelopes after the envelope has been printed, there will most likely be an additional charge for this service. Mailers who use an outside vendor to apply addresses and bar codes to their mailing pieces often use the keycode method.

Colored marker method

Development shops that mail in small quantities can identify campaigns by color coding envelopes on the side with a colored felt marker (approximately a 1-1.5 inch stack of envelopes at a time). This method is less efficient than key coding and does have its disadvantages. However, it also does provide a means to gather information for purposes of evaluation.

When this method is used, you must be careful to insure that the side of each envelope is inked so that upon its return, the data-entry staff will have no difficulty distinguishing its color code. This method works well for small shops that use the same envelope in a variety of campaigns. Its disadvantage is that occasionally the ink will not penetrate the side of the envelope and its return will be unrecorded as a result. Additionally, the colored marks do need to be applied by hand, therefore it is cost-effective only in small quantities, or where quality control with volunteers is assured.

Colored dot

This method appears more professional than the above method. However, it also requires more staff time to ensure that each dot sticker is applied correctly in the corner of the envelope.

Bar-coding

Bar-coding is a system of optical characters that can be electronically recognized by machine. These codes are printed on price tags and grocery items to expedite processing of sales and on envelopes to expedite mail processing.

Bar-coding can be used in many other ways. It can be used to track product inventory. Many organizations that receive many donations on a daily basis often use a bar-code scanner to expedite data-entry for gift recording. This method also minimizes the probability of errors as well as the staff time required for the job. Setting up such a system does require purchase of a scanner to read the bar-code and a software program that converts the code into the proper format for entry into your data track-

ing system. However, if your organization is entering a large number of gifts several days each week, it will be well worth the cost.

Bar-coding is the most time-efficient method of evaluating the results of your mailing campaigns. An important benefit offered by bar-coding is that it allows you to code the account where the donation will be entered in your data management system, as well as any other pertinent information relating to the donor.

Is Direct Mail Appropriate for Your Organization?

Direct mail is an effective tool to educate individuals about your programs and services and secure their financial support. Direct mail acquisition campaigns can also make it possible for you to secure new donors or members.

Direct mail packages normally consist of a letter to your donor or prospect, a reply device (separate card or tear-off portion of donor envelope), an informational brochure about your programs and services (optional), a donor remittance envelope, and an outer envelope for mailing the package.

Books, articles, and professional direct marketing firms can provide you with more details about how to develop your package, identify your mailing list, and handle fulfillment of the donor's gift. While this book will not explain in detail the technicalities of a direct mail program, we will provide information to help you evaluate the use of direct mail fund raising as well as the essential components required for success.

Consider cost

Initially, direct mail acquisition campaigns are capital intensive. Initial returns on acquisition campaigns for new donors or members usually average between a one-half percent to two percent response. Most organizations discover that, depending upon the campaign's scope and design, the cost to acquire a donor or member may run from $1.00 to $20.00. Although some organizations may break even, this is really an exception rather than the rule. The real benefit to your organization comes through subsequent mailings as donors begin to upgrade and repeat their giving.

It normally will take three years or more before you begin to see significant revenues from your direct mail campaign. By this time, if you have been managing your donors effectively, you will have begun to see some major gifts. If you wait for seven to ten years, you will probably receive a planned gift or capital gift.

This is the advantage of direct mail. As a source for individual gifts, it can provide steady operating, capital, or special gift support for an organization. Therefore, if your organization intends to reap the full benefits from direct mail fund raising, you must be prepared to wait. Equally important is that you must be prepared to commit the necessary resources in order to regularly communicate with your donors and to cultivate their interest and gifts throughout the years.

Next, we would like to discuss a number of things you can do in order to reduce your costs and increase campaign results.

Effectively Written Copy is Essential

The written message you share with your donors and prospects will garner their interest and support. You may wish to write the copy for the letter, return device, and brochure. However, be aware that unless you, a staff member, or a volunteer has skills in this area, it may, in the long term, prove to be more costly to your organization than if you hire a professional writer. Unless you are skilled in direct-mail copy writing, you may wish only to provide information and conceptual ideas to the copy writer. Or, you may wish to write the draft and allow the copy writer to fine tune the letter, developing it specifically for a direct mail audience.

Timing and Frequency

The time of year you conduct your direct mail campaign and how often you contact donors and donor prospects depends on your organization's cash flow needs, budget, and ability to handle the logistics of a direct mail program. A successful direct mail program requires that you communicate with your donors at least three or four times yearly. Because today's market is so competitive, if you do not maintain your relationship, some other organization will. As well, if you have campaigns that do not do well, consider changing the time of year for the mail date, along with changes in copy, content, and design.

Consider Management Costs

Many vendors offer services for small organizations in personalized letter preparation, bulk mail preparation, copy writing, mail management, fulfillment, and database management. By using outside vendors, you can extend the capabilities of your organization without having to train staff or secure costly equipment. Check with other nonprofit organizations to see who is reputable in your area.

Consider the cost-effectiveness of having retiree groups or corporations help you assemble your bulk mail. However, remember that today's requirements for bulk mail are becoming more technical in nature. If you decide to use these groups, you must be prepared to train them in proper mail preparation.

Donor Acknowledgment

The timing and manner in which you thank your donors is just as important as the mailing itself. Donor revenues are maximized from subsequent contributions. It is very important that your donors' gifts are acknowledged and that the acknowledgment is sent within a short time after the gift is received. Professional direct marketing services can provide fulfillment services, some at reasonable cost. Or, some organizations have volunteers sign and send preprinted gift acknowledgment cards to smaller donors while individualized personal letters signed by the executive director or board chairperson are sent to larger donors.

The signer on the acknowledgment is not as important as the need to acknowledge your donors in a timely manner. Additional ideas for donor acknowledgment are found in Chapter 9.

Everything You Ever Wanted to Know about Lists

An indispensable ingredient in a successful donor/member acquisition campaign is the selection of the prospect list. However, list purchase or rental can be an expensive proposition for small development programs. How can you be resourceful with a limited budget?

How to Secure Names/Lists for Prospecting

There are a number of alternatives that minimize the number of lists you must purchase. The easiest thing to do is to work closely with your house file to try to retain your active donors, members, and purchasers. This can be done by communicating frequently and designing communications that will appeal to their personal interests.

Yet, it still will be essential to prospect in order to maintain current revenue levels. This is because even the most well-managed program will lose approximately 25% of its donors or members from year to year.

As you look at securing names from other sources, here are a few ideas to try:

■ Acquire names of prospects from inserts in newspapers and magazines.

■ Use call-in membership information publicity programs on radio and television.

■ Secure names of donors and prospects from coupons inserted with products (perhaps there is a business that serves the same clientele.)

■ Get referrals from satisfied clients or purchasers.

Every year, you can try a number of different ideas or promotions to expand your database. Rely on your own creativity to develop marketing strategies to help you beat the perpetually shrinking database.

One way is to ask your staff, board, and volunteers for their mailing lists of family, friends, and co-workers. Secure lists of people who attend your open houses and special events, or those who inquire about your organization. Borrow or trade lists with other organizations. (Be sure to inquire as to whether there are any regulations that prohibit this in your state.)

When using these methods to acquire lists it is important to always track the source of names on a list and to track the subsequent results from the list. One way of doing this is to use a field within the database structure designated as 'source' so that you will know the origin. The date of first entry into the file is also important. Of course, you may also keep lists separate by using diskettes or tapes. In this manner you will be able to discard lists or names that have not proven to be good prospecting tools.

When borrowing lists you should also consider how well they perform. Even if you obtain a free list, you will still pay the costs of mailing and production. If a free list performs poorly, it actually may be more costly to your organization than paying for lists that are suited more specifically to your purpose. Here are a few thoughts when considering the use of lists.

Which Lists Are Best to Use?

Which lists are best? The answer is: it depends. Generally, your goal should be to try to match the list to the purpose and concept of the offer or solicitation. In other words, if you are staging a fund raising telethon for a battered women's shelter, then one of your lists should be "responders to domestic abuse appeals who contributed by phone." If such a list is not available or if you have trouble filling the order with enough names from a particular list, then you might try your next best alternatives. You could also try lists of contributors who have contributed by mail to women's causes, subscribers to a women's

---

Case Example

A human service organization that served the homeless used a total of three mailing lists. One was a compiled list (a list of names without response characteristics) and the other two were response lists (a list of names of those who have actually responded to an appeal), of donors to related causes. To their surprise, the compiled list outperformed the other two lists in terms of response rate.
Later evaluation determined that the people on the compiled list had already been mailed to earlier in the year, whereas the response lists had been mailed just once. Thus, it made sense that the compiled list might perform better; the prospects were more informed about the organization because they had received two communications instead of one.

---

magazine, or contributors to general causes.

With the latest technology available to select names on the basis of demographics or life-styles, compiled lists are now performing better. Compiled lists are those that are "compiled" of individuals who meet a certain characteristic. They differ from "response lifts" which are lists of individuals who have responded to certain types of appeals, such as telemarketing or direct mail. If you think that you have some ideas about the demographic or life-style characteristics of your best prospects, then using a compiled list, with this information appended on the basis of these selective variables, is also a possibility. We will discuss this topic in greater detail under the topic: *How to Expand the Number of Lists Available through Database Segmentation.*

Choosing the right list is more of an art than a science. Sometimes results do not always turn out the way you expect. Sometimes a list will work well for one particular purpose and fail miserably in another. This is why professionals who purchase lists are always testing, testing, testing.

How to Determine Which Lists are Best, or TESTING 1-2-3

The only way to know really which lists are better than others is to test different lists. In this manner you will spread the risk on every mailing. If you order only one list and that list fails miserably, then you will be in bigger trouble than if you used three lists and only one list failed. In the latter case, at least you would have had reasonable results from two of the three lists.

To have a reasonably valid test, you will need to order a minimum of 5,000 names. Because of the laws of statistics, the greater your sample size, the less the margin of error. Thus, results from a test run with 10,000 names will be more predictable than results from a test that was run with 5,000 names.

Questions to Ask When Purchasing a List

What is the list source? Magazine subscriptions? Space ads? People who have called in or registered for classes?

Are they actual donors or survey respondents? Survey respondents may include those who have answered yes to a question on a survey asking them if they had made a charitable contribution in the last year. This information is considered *soft* data, whereas an actual donor record is *hard* data, based on an actual occurrence rather than the vagaries of someone's memory.

Is it taken from direct mail or telemarketing lists? Donors responsive to telemarketing solicitations may or may not be responsive to mail campaigns and vice versa.

Does the list contain names of active donors, names of prospects or both? This is an extremely important question. You may ask how long it has been since the donor contributed or since the purchaser actually made a purchase of certain merchandise.

What is the average unit of sale or average donation (for fund raising or product sale lists)?
This refers to the average product dollar purchase or the average contribution size. Relate this information to your campaign. If you will be offering high price gift opportunities, it may be wise to test a list known to have a higher donation amount (or unit of sale.)

Is the list a response list or is it a compiled list?
A compiled list contains only a list of names compiled from one or more sources. A response list contains names of people who actually have responded to an offer or solicitation.

How frequently has the list been serviced at NCOA?
NCOA stands for National Change of Address operated by the United States Post Office. Most list managers who advertise in *Standard Rate*

and Data Service (SRDS) will clean their lists quarterly. *(Standard Rate and Data Service* is a publication used by list managers and list brokers to advertise lists.) It is an additional advantage, of course, if the list is cleaned on a monthly basis to eliminate incorrect or duplicate addresses.

Does the list manager guarantee deliverability?
Mailers usually guarantee anywhere from 85 percent to 95 percent deliverability. What this means is that if you keep track of the addresses that are not delivered, you will be reimbursed for those names, when you return the undelivered letters to the list manager. However, it is unlikely that you will find a list company willing to reimburse for the other costs associated with mailing the piece.

Is the list related to the appeal?
Naturally, you don't want to sell wool socks to residents of southern Florida. There are some lists that will perform well for you and you will not know what the exact connection is. However, you generally will have better results if you choose lists that seem to have an apparent connection with the appeal.

What are the costs of this list compared to others?
Lists may vary in price depending upon the desirability of the list.

What other organizations or businesses have rented this list?

A list manager or owner should provide you with this information, most frequently in written form.

Are there a large number of duplicated names?

This seems likely if you've used this list before or have merged the list with your house list. If there are, chances are that the composition of the list is similar to your house file. This is a positive sign!

What is the roll-out quantity?

Just a fancy way of saying: what is the total number of names on the list that fit your specifications?

Can labels be applied by machine?

Some lists are only available on pressure-sensitive labels, which need to be applied by hand. Most lists available on the commercial market are available on magnetic tape or diskette.

Are pledge or order cards available for telemarketing?

Many vendors will provide printed cards, at additional charge, for your staff and volunteers to use when conducting telemarketing campaigns.

How recent are the names?

Some list managers offer a hotline. These are individuals who have responded within the last three to six months.

What selections are available?

Can certain portions of the list be selected or is it necessary to order a minimum quantity? (A normal minimum quantity is 5,000 names.) This is important if you wish to order only those individuals within a certain income range, zip code, or geographical region.

How many other organizations are ordering continuation mailings?

Note that this is a different question than how many others have rented the list. An organization that is doing cost-effective direct mail usually will only order enough names to test the validity of a list. As mentioned earlier in this chapter, the quantities necessary for a reasonable test are 5,000-10,000. Then, if the list performs well for the initial test, the buyer will order more names for what is known as a roll out. You should inquire about how many people are ordering roll out quantities after testing. This is also known as continuation.

Will the list manager guarantee the delivery date?

If you feel pretty sure that a list is going to perform for you, you can ask the list manager or broker to guarantee a delivery date in the future. Many list owners want to know who is mailing to their list and some may even limit the number of times that their house list can be used by other sources. To prevent the likelihood that your chosen list will be unavailable, it's best to guarantee a date.

How many on the list use credit cards? How many have phone numbers?

This is important if you would like to do an integrated campaign, such as telemarketing along with a mail campaign. Although it is possible to append phone numbers to a list, it is usually more cost effective to order a list with phone numbers, all other factors remaining equal.

How Do You Eliminate the Possibility of Mailing to the Same People More Than Once?

Most organizations that are heavy mailers will use 10-20 lists at any given time. When you use this many lists, it is not uncommon to have a high duplication rate, particularly if you are targeting a limited area. It is equally important, if you are doing a prospect mailing for new donors, that you remove any of your donors' names that may be included on the purchased list, before the mailing is sent to donor prospects. Upon receiving the magnetic tapes from all of your list sources, your mail house can do a merge-purge to eliminate duplicates and to suppress any house file names from the list to be mailed.

How Much Time Do You Need to Order Lists?

On some survey and compiled lists, you may complete an order and receive it by overnight mail with a two- to three-day turnaround. Gener-

ally, however, the list purchasing process takes much longer. If you give your list broker some lead time (at least 30 days), he or she can shop around for the best lists available. (Some list owners "block out" certain mail dates when they will be using the list for their own mailings.) Also, you will want to allow a couple of weeks in order to get your mail pieces approved, should your list owner wish to exercise this option. Additionally, you will want to allow time at the mail house for the merge-purge process. In consideration of all the time necessary for these items, you may wish to plan your list orders up to six months before your actual mail date.

When Is the Best Time to Mail to Your List?

The Direct Marketing Association tracks the number of mailings every year. What they have discovered in their surveys of thousands of mailers is that prospecting mailings are done at all times of the year. There are a number of factors to consider when timing a mailing. It's true that many individuals do tend to make charitable contributions at the end of the calendar year. However, the months of November and December are extremely heavy mail volume months. Thus, you will have more competition if you mail during this time of year.

Because of this, many mailers also conduct prospect campaigns in

January through April. The best thing to do is to arrive at a schedule that works for your organization and complete testing at two or three different times of the year.

Should You Rent Out Your House List to Others?

If you have 5,000 or more names in your house list, you are in a position to consider renting or exchanging your list with another organization. There are many different opinions as to whether this is a good idea. Some organizations feel that to allow others to use their list will endanger their chances of maintaining their clients or donors. The only flaw in this logic is that these donors probably are being mailed solicitations from many other organizations anyway. Today, there is such a proliferation of mail communications, the likelihood of donor prospects receiving other appeals is quite high.

For example, anyone with a social security number will appear on many lists. Usually people who are mail responsive often appear on more than one list. Today's technology allows tracking of individuals from many different sources.

Thus, if they are being mailed to by other parties anyway, why not allow yourself to obtain the list rental income from these mailings? List rental can supplement your organization's income or help you pay for your own prospecting lists. Some organizations actually tell their donors that their names will not be sold or rented to anyone else. This is fine as long as the organization does not change its mind at some later date. Be sure to check on state laws or regulations that may prohibit the sale, rental, or exchange of nonprofit mailing lists in your state. If, however, you do decide to rent or exchange your list, the next thing to consider is whether you will handle the operation yourself.

Although it is possible to rent your list yourself, you may be better off having a list broker help you. A list broker will provide additional exposure to possible renters, and will assist you in making sure that your list is in the best possible shape for rental. He or she should also assist you with setting up the correct formats and in executing the orders as requested by the list customers.

Your list broker should also help you protect your list from fraudulent practices. One of the ways that list owners protect their list is by seeding the list with their own name or that of friends. If you misspell these names and receive a mailing you have not anticipated, then you will know who is mailing to you unofficially.

Many marketing firms provide list brokerage services. A publication at your local library, *Standard Rate and Data Service,* contains a listing of many of these companies.

Cutting Your Mailing Costs by Effective File Management

National Change of Address

There's an old adage among fund raisers: if you're not cleaning your database, then you're losing donors. On average, up to 15 percent of the clients or donors in your house (organization) file will change their addresses during the year. If you mail first-class, for a short period of time the Postal Service will forward mail to the individual's new address. Although this gets your mail forwarded, it does not make the corrections to your house database. Moreover, if you're like most nonprofit organizations, you mail third class to save money. Because third-class postage does not include the services of address-correction or forwarding, you will not be notified of these changes unless you pay for the additional services of "ADDRESS CORRECTION REQUESTED" or NATIONAL CHANGE OF ADDRESS, two services that are offered by the U. S. Postal Service. Consequently, you eventually will lose track of a certain number of individuals over time.

If you are a very small mailer, or if the piece that you are sending is very important, you can use the ADDRESS CORRECTION REQUESTED service. This is stamped below your return address on the exterior envelope. Each incorrect address is returned to you with the correct address attached, for a service fee of approximately 35 cents each. However, most organizations that mail 2,000 or more pieces per year at the third-class rate will find it more economical to use NATIONAL CHANGE OF ADDRESS service (NCOA.)

For the first time only, the post office will correct the addresses and append zip codes in your database free of charge. After this, with a nominal fee (usually only $200 - $300 for a file of 10,000 names), you can have an outside vendor correct your addresses, including mail carrier routes, zip-codes, or zip-fours. Sometimes the savings in postage just from adding zip-fours may be worth using NATIONAL CHANGE OF ADDRESS.

These services are usually contracted through a computer-based service bureau which will issue a CASS CERTIFICATION that enables you to receive postal discounts for a period of six months to one year. The CASS CERTIFICATION (Form 3553) notifies the postal service that your database is organized in such a way that it is easy to identify, sort, and deliver. At the time of this printing, rules for nonprofit organizations are currently under review, so check with your local postal authority to verify requirements.

An excellent guide for mailers, *Mailroom Companion,* can be obtained free of charge from the U.S. Postal Service, Address Quality, 6060 Primacy Pky # 201, Memphis, TN 38188-0001.

Automation Compatible Mail

In the future, the United States Postal Service will offer more discounts for mailers who have automation compatible mail. It is absolutely essential that you consider how to make your mail automation compatible. "Automation compatible" means that your mail will have a barcode that can be read with an optical scanner.

Many software programs are able to apply delivery point barcodes that are recognized by the postal service. Your local post office business mail department will supply you with the names of some software programs that have bar-codes that are acceptable for use in the mail. Unfortunately, the price for many software packages on this list can run several hundred dollars.

One less expensive alternative is that Microsoft *Word* ® will also print an 11-digit delivery point barcode. This option appears in the menu when you print labels. Another option would be to get a mailing program software. Some are available for as little as $100. The important thing to remember is to first of all, get your list CASS CERTIFIED every six months in order to qualify for the lowest postal discounts.

If you have trouble printing the barcode with your system, the problem may be your printer. This is unusual however, most barcode programs support the standard laser or dot-matrix printers.

Some individuals do not wish to manage their own mail programs. If you would prefer to use outside vendors, or are unable to apply barcodes to your mail, you may wish to use an outside mail preparation vendor. There is usually only a nominal fee for this service. These fees will frequently will be recouped in the savings accrued through automation discounts. The amount of savings depends on the quantity of mail being processed.

Deceased File

Currently, four list companies provide services that correct the records of deceased individuals in a specific file. These correction filters are compiled from nixies (nondeliverables), obituary records, and social security files. When this list is used, it usually eliminates an additional one-to-two percent of records that is no longer useful. Check with list brokers, mail preparation firms or marketing firms to arrange for such a service.

Technology in Marketing Management

Technology is changing so quickly. As you read this chapter, the technologies described may have been upgraded or replaced by more modern and efficient systems. The costs of technology are also changing rapidly, bringing exciting new possibilities within reach of your organization.

Consider using technology to improve your marketing and development. A moderately sophisticated database program will enable you to identify and track key variables for improved decisions. Tracking will help you improve the effectiveness of your key strategies. Refer to chapter 5 for more in-depth information about developing segmentation strategies based on information variables.

By analyzing zipcodes, you may be able to determine which areas of your community are more receptive to your programming or fund raising appeals.

Similarly, tracking expenses and revenues from individual campaigns will enable you to observe which campaigns are most cost effective per dollar raised.

Analyze the demographics of your donors, clients, and members. What are their income levels, ethnic background, and or educational levels? This information will assist you in choosing media. It will also help you to develop your copy platforms.

Age is also an extremely important variable. If you are communicating by letter with an audience over the age of 60, you may wish to use large type. Recent studies indicate that, for people over the age of 70, mail responsiveness appears to decline significantly. Therefore, you may even wish to consider alternative types of communication vehicles with these individuals, such as video or phone.

Education and ethnic background are also critical variables. Educational level impacts communication needs in many ways. Depending on level of interest and education, highly educated donors may want and need more detailed descriptions of your programs, including financial data. Lastly, income data is used by many organizations. This is a sensitive issue however, because all individuals give, regardless of income level. However, those at higher levels of income are capable of giving more. Additionally, there are many individuals who might be ranked as having lower income levels, such as senior citizens, yet who actually may have high levels of assets in savings, bonds, and/or real estate. Therefore income level alone is not an accurate indicator of total wealth.

Many organizations are reluctant to set up tracking systems or to evaluate informational variables. Perhaps you

157

might be saying "It's just not possible for us to collect this much information." or "It just seems like too much work." Yet, even if you can start in some small way to begin to collect data, it will improve your results. Once you discover how to use this information, you may choose to enlarge your data-gathering systems.

Some organizations rely upon an outside vendor to manage their data. This type of data gathering is certainly better than no data gathering at all. Yet, what would happen if the database was lost by the firm? Most marketing firms will not use names that belong to another organization. Yet, the only way that you can guarantee the security of your house file is to manage it yourself. Furthermore, donors and funding sources may inquire about the demographics of your constituents. If you maintain this information, you will be prepared to answer these questions.

Above all, this file is the lifeblood of your organization. As such it should be guarded with the utmost care. If you have not already made backup files of your database files do so today!

How to Expand the Number of Lists Through Database Segmentation

Have you reached a point in your prospecting where you feel that you have run out of lists to try? It's not difficult to run out of fund raising lists because the number of donor response lists is a finite universe. Some mailers whose geographic target area is limited reach a saturation point very quickly. If this has happened to you, then it is time to try some other list-expansion tricks.

Earlier in this chapter we discussed the options available in terms of selects for a file. The use of these selects allows you to take what normally would be considered a mediocre list, and turn it into a list that performs quite well. For example, let us suppose that your organization provides services to pet owners. Does this mean that all pet owners will respond to your appeal? It is not likely. If you have any information about what type of individual is most likely to respond, however, you can enhance your list through the demographic or life-style selection process.

Let us say that you suspect that females, age 45 and older, are the main constituents within your house file. These are two possible selection variables. And, although demographics are extremely important, there are other, equally important variables. Many marketing firms have a comprehensive array of survey information compiled on thousands of individuals. These surveys secure information using many methods; product cards, warranty registration, and subscription information. Usually list brokers or marketing professionals know which suppliers can select on these variables. They also know what computer service firms might provide special services in data selection or manipulation.

For example, let us presume that you have been provided with a list by one of your nonprofit colleagues. You know nothing about this list other than the name of the organization to which it belongs. What you do know, however, is what donor characteristics or types of individuals have responded well to your past appeals. (In order to mail effectively you should try to obtain information about your best donors or clients on a regular basis.) If you are a heavy mailer, this information is extremely valuable. It is so valuable, that some mailers use predictive modeling techniques on their house list in order to obtain demographic or psychographic information.

These techniques are based on the use of multivariate statistical models to identify what characteristics are predictive of future behavior. Just think, if you knew that your best donors or members were females, age 50 and older, without children in the household, how much more effective you could be in targeting your appeals! You would also know how to choose lists.

A number of different modeling techniques can be used to gather data about the individuals in your house file. In addition to predictive modeling, you may gather data for information purposes only. This is an important distinction to remember. The modeling techniques that rely upon multivariate statistics are predictive in nature, rather than information that may be appended (or added to fields) within your house file. Just because an individual is expected to have certain characteristics does not mean that they will perform the desired behaviors.

Nonetheless, any time that you can gain more information about the individuals in your database it will improve your strategy development. You will be able to make more informed judgements as to whether telemarketing and/or specialized premium offers will be well received. As well, you may be able to learn whether they enjoy travel, sports, and/or other activities to help you design more appropriate special events.

You can significantly enhance lists by using these techniques to select individuals who meet certain criteria from an overall list. This will allow you to minimize the number of direct mail packages that you would need to mail. Two variables that are useful for fund raising mailings are "volunteerism" and "participation in volunteer activities".

Unfortunately, not every list owner or manager will collect this information in their database. By using service vendors that specialize in these overlay techniques, however, you can obtain more information about the characteristics of any list.

Appending Information To The Database

Many organizations receive contributions from individuals. With the trend towards personalization, communication with individuals is becoming more and more sophisticated. Managers ask: are these individuals young, old, female, male, or at what educational or income level? Knowing these key variables significantly improves the ability to communicate more effectively. See Chapter 2, *Prospect Research*.

Fortunately, there are many marketing services available today that will append, or add, information to an organization's house file. CACI Marketing Systems, and Donnelly, Inc., are two companies that will provide such a service. These companies use sophisticated clustering techniques to organize data and information about an individual.

The result is that individuals are grouped into a certain *cluster.* CACI uses the ACORN system which includes such clusters as:

- Up and Coming Singles
- Affluent Families
- Upper Income Empty Nesters
- Settled Southwestern Hispanics
- Top One-Percent

Naturally, the validity of this clustering process is only as valuable as the underlying data which helps to form the cluster designations. Nearly all systems use census data and telephone and credit card data. However, some companies have more extensive modeling and data gathering processes. Often, an organization will retain a marketing consultant to assist the organization in selecting the right company and services, depending on needs and objectives. A wide range of costs and/or services are possible.

The procedure itself is simple: an organization sends a copy of its appropriate house data base on diskette or magnetic tape to the marketing service firm for this process. Development staff may fear that the service firm will use the names for their own purposes. This is certainly not a normal occurrence. It is unethical for these firms to use the names on your data base for any other purpose. Nonetheless, development managers should always confirm this with a marketing service vendor before using their services.

The data that is most frequently appended to files includes:

- SCF (Sectional Center Facility, a major mailing center for the United States Postal Service. The SCF is the first three numbers of the zip-code)
- Zip-code, county, and state
- Carrier route
- Zip-4
- Telephone number
- Block group
- Age of head of household
- Age of individual
- Gender
- Education
- Income (estimated)
- Credit card usage
- Dwelling unit type
- Mail responsiveness
- Presence and age of children
- Purchasing habits
- Field of study and school type (for colleges and universities)
- Religious and ethnic surnames (Catholic, Jewish, and Hispanic).

Profitable Marketing and Fund Raising Ideas

Memorial and Tribute Programs

Offering donors an opportunity to make a gift to your organization in the name of a friend or loved one is an ideal way in which to honor an individual, increase public awareness, and generate revenues.

Memorial and tribute donor packages normally consist of a donor card and envelope, or space for donor information printed on the envelope. Donors may use the program to memorialize someone who has died or pay tribute to someone who is celebrating a birthday, anniversary, graduation, bar mitzvah, birth, or other special occasion. When the organization receives the memorial or tribute gift, they send out a special card to the person or family being recognized. This recognizes the gift and also permits the organization to explain its mission and programs to a new audience. In addition, when the organization sends an acknowledgment to the donor it may include an additional memorial and tribute donor package to encourage the donor to make an additional gift.

Donor/Member Premiums

Premium programs offer donors and members an incentive to make a first-time or upgraded gift. Research indicates that individuals are more likely to respond to premium-based solicitations. Therefore, depending on the goals and budget of your development program, they are worth considering. As you develop your ideas for donor premiums, keep the following in mind:

- Individuals who respond to premium-based solicitations often need to be renewed and upgraded through similar premium-based solicitations.

■ Premiums advertised in the mail must be closely related to your organization's mission or they will not qualify for nonprofit rates. In addition, the income you gain through the offer of donor premiums could be interpreted by the Internal Revenue Service as unrelated business income.

■ New rules require nonprofit organizations to report to donors the value of any premiums. Current legislation considers any premium having a fair market value of $6.50 or less as inconsequential. However, any premiums offered as an incentive to donors having a greater market value must be so stated to the donor.

Although premiums may be used in many ways, they are most commonly used in direct response (mail and/or telephone solicitation) and major gifts.

Direct Response

Nonprofit organizations can effectively use calendars, bookmarks, decorative stamps, address labels, and other insertions as a response incentive. These may be either *front end* premiums, (inserted in the solicitation) or *back end* premiums (mailed after the respondent has sent in the required funds.)

When considering the use of premiums, it is wise to calculate the economies of mass purchases, as well as the type of premiums that correspond with the mission of your organization. Purchasing in bulk may enable you to negotiate wholesale prices or allow you to design your own personalized version of a stock premium. Another appropriate option for educational organizations is to develop publications and videos.

Whatever premium you may choose, it is helpful to convene a focus group of your target audience or survey them by phone or mail as to their impressions of the premium. Although responses to such a survey are apt to be varied and cannot guarantee an accurate prediction, you will still gather critical information to help you consider various types of premiums as well as their relative advantages.

Giving Clubs (Major Gifts)

Premiums are also used to increase the size of donor or member gifts. Normally, premium-based solicitations of this nature are sent to individuals who give at the $50 level and above. (They can be sent to donors at the $25 level, but generally the rate of response will be less.)

It is best to develop a specifically targeted package, offered by mail or phone, for this purpose. The package should detail the benefits to the donor at various gift levels. Usually a highly visual package offering higher quality premiums yields better results. Here again it is best to first survey a sample group of your target audience to determine what premiums and sales messages might be most appealing. Gift club acknowledgments are discussed in Chapter 9, *Donor Acknowledgments and Recognition.*

Telemarketing

Telemarketing allows an organization to contact donors and prospects personally when it is not feasible to actually meet with them. It is the "next best thing to being there."

People often complain about the intrusiveness of a charity calling them at home and asking for their support. Still, telemarketing remains one of the most effective ways to secure the support of donors and to identify new donor prospects.

Telemarketing can be used in a variety of ways. It can be used to solicit donors, thank them for their past contributions, survey them about the organization's programs or services, notify them of an upcoming event, and invite them to become a volunteer.

Case Example

A prominent national brokerage firm has trained its brokers to make cold calls by having them do fund raising telemarketing for area nonprofit organizations. Selected nonprofit groups provide background information and an orientation to the broker trainees. The organizations also work closely with the brokerage training staff to develop a telephone script that accurately portrays the mission of the organizations, presents a clear case for support and offers prospective donors opportunities for supporting the organizations. Trainees call prospective or lapsed donors over the period of four to six weeks. This no-cost telemarketing effort creates a win-win situation where the brokers and the charitable groups benefit from the program.

A telemarketing program can be a costly proposition for a small non-profit organization. However, many professional telemarketing firms can effectively generate contributions from current and new donors that more than break even with the costs of their efforts. It is important to research telemarketing firms, get references from other organizations, and find a firm that supports your mission. You should use a firm that will be a sensitive and positive representative for your organization.

To reduce costs many organizations use volunteers and staff to conduct their telemarketing efforts. Using phones within an organization's office or a donated phone bank at a local business or firm, volunteer telemarketing programs can be just as effective as those of a professional service. However, the key to success is selecting motivated volunteers who can speak well on the telephone. You must also provide training and support materials including a script outline. Practice role playing and encourage a team effort so that volunteers can work together to share their successes and failures.

In every volunteer telemarketing program it is essential to maintain motivation and attitude. It's important to make this a fun job, because the callers will face rejection again and again. Provide small gifts or bonuses to the top callers, the top gift, or the most calls completed.

Give awards and plenty of praise. Inform them that it is part of the job to face rejection and that the number of objections that a caller faces only brings them closer to their goal. The training process should include sample phrases for how to overcome caller objections, while still maintaining the donor or member relationship. You might even bring in an accomplished sales person to help them understand the "selling process" of overcoming objections.

Above all, callers should always be considerate of donor or member wishes. The caller should first ask if it is an appropriate time to talk or if the caller should call again later. The reason why telemarketing carries such negative connotations is that many solicitors do not respect the wishes of the donor or member. As well, many calls are received late in the evening or during the dinner hour. Be watchful of these items.

It helps to have easy-to-read script materials, like the sample pledge chart shown in Illustration 20. Instruct the caller to ask a donor for more than their last gift--up to four times more, if the donor has a long gift history. A description of what each gift level will accomplish is also helpful. For membership campaigns, a description of the membership benefits is appropriate.

Also, make it easy for the donor to give. A telemarketing program needs

Illustration 20: Telemarketing Pledge Chart

Community Youth Service Agency

Ask for:	Make it manageable	Break it down	Other ideas
$150	$75 semi-annually $37.50 quarterly	Less than $3.00 per week Less than 50 cents per day	Tax-deductible
$100	$50 semi-annually $25 quarterly	Less than $2.00 per week Less than 30 cents per day	Provides one camp scholarship
$75	$37.50 semi-annually	Less than $1.50 per week	Provides one counseling session to a troubled kid
$50	$25.00 semi-annually	Less than $1.00 per week	The cost of books for parent support groups
$25	One payment only	Less than 50 cents per week Less than 8 cents per day	Provides meals for one child for one week
$15	One payment only	Less than 30 cents per day	Provides membership for one child in program

to be able to accept credit card pledges over the phone to ensure the contribution of the donor. The next best option is to send a pledge reminder and contribution envelope as a follow-up to a donor's pledge. It is not uncommon to have to send three or four reminders in order to fulfill 75%-90% of the pledges obtained.

The least successful approach is to use only one pledge reminder communication. This usually results in a dramatic reduction in gifts obtained.

In telemarketing campaigns, callers should always be considerate of donor or member wishes.

Matching Gifts

Corporations who match gifts of their employees' charitable contributions offer nonprofit organizations an opportunity to double or even triple the amount of a donor's gift. Hundreds of corporations throughout the country support their employees' charitable interests through matching gifts from the corporation's or foundation's assets. Some companies even match gifts given by an employee's spouse and by retirees of the company.

How can a small development shop take advantage of matching gift programs? Ask! Ask your donors in your newsletters, annual reports, direct mail solicitations, and telemarketing campaigns to find out if their company will match their charitable gifts. One of the easiest ways to accomplish this is to add a simple line to your reply device in all of your contribution forms, or mail reply devices asking the donors to have their employer match their gift, if possible.

Additionally, if you know of certain corporations that match gifts to your organization, you may also preprint the names of these businesses on a separate communication insert included with your contribution request. This offers the additional advantage of allowing employees to see their company named as an actual matching gift sponsor. Still, there are many companies who match gifts that are not generally known to most nonprofit organizations. The actual mechanics of executing the match require the donor to complete a brief form and send it to your organization for confirmation of the receipt of their gift. Your organization then returns it to the corporation for processing of the matching gift check.

A listing of national matching gift companies can be obtained through:

Council for Advancement and Support of Education (CASE)
Suite 400
11 Dupont Circle
Washington DC 20036

Matching gifts can generate substantial support for your organization. In addition to the financial value, a matching gifts program may also increase awareness of your organization by corporations in your community, thus enhancing your ability to generate additional corporate gifts in the future. Many corporations today are practicing what has been coined as "the democratization of fund raising." They donate to organizations which their employees support and work as active volunteers. By promoting matching gifts for your organization you can make corporations more aware of the support you are receiving from their employees and in turn encourage corporate support of your organization's mission and programs.

"Marriage Mail" Programs

Another easy and economical means of getting your message and return device into the hands of individuals is "marriage mail." This is a group of businesses or nonprofit organizations sharing the costs of list purchase and mailing to reach a wide audience in a specified geographical area.

You may receive "marriage mail" and not even realize it. You may view it as a form of "junk mail" but it has proven successful for some organizations, generally those with some degree of name recognition. It is delivered as a packet of individual ads for local businesses, pizza delivery, or mail order opportunities. Sometimes the package may arrive in the form of a card deck of ads from numerous organizations, businesses, and services.

Response rates for this type of advertising are generally less than that of direct mail acquisition, in the range of less than two percent.

In some communities, many nonprofit organizations put together their own individual inserts into a charity package of perhaps 20 to 30 charities that is then sent to community residents as an informational and prospecting tool.

Prices vary widely for this type of advertising. Media companies in your area may offer special rates and opportunities to nonprofit organizations. They may also offer you opportunities for free space in their inserts when they have a last-minute cancellation by an advertiser. The opportunity for you to get your organization's message into the hands of hundreds of thousands of community residents at no cost is certainly worth pursuing. You may wish to track results for three or four offerings before making a permanent buying decision.

Piggyback Programs

Often a large-scale mailer will allow a nonprofit organization to insert promotional material into their own mail packages, with little or no charge. Cable and utility companies are excellent candidates because they execute a huge number of mailings

"Marriage mail" programs allow nonprofit organizations an opportunity to share the costs of list purchase and mailing to reach a wide audience in the community in a very cost effective manner.

167

throughout a wide area. When participating in such a program you will want to consider whether you wish to pay a possible shared mailing cost if the mailing is being distributed to an area that your organization does not serve. However, the mailer may be willing to allow you to insert your mailing piece in only those pre-selected zip-codes that match your target geographic area.

Newspaper Inserts

A common means of business advertising, but one seldom used by nonprofit organizations is special inserts in local newspapers. This marketing technique can be used to announce an upcoming event on a one-page flier, offer cause-related marketing coupons to the reader, or deliver an informational brochure and gift opportunity.

For a small development shop, newspaper inserts may also offer a unique opportunity for underwriting by a corporate sponsor, which could pay for the costs of the insert through its advertising budget.

Further, newspaper inserts allow you to target certain geographic areas within the newspaper's circulation. Some organizations find them to be more cost-effective than direct mail because the initial investment is often less.

More New Ideas from the Field

Food Shelf Card Program

Many organizations use card programs for memorial/tribute giving. In this program the organization mails a greeting card or premium to an individual who is honored by a gift to the organization from another individual. An organization in Minneapolis, Minnesota, took this idea one step further. It encouraged donors to use the card program at Christmas and Mother's Day, when the majority of greeting cards are purchased. By offering to mail cards to individuals' entire mailing lists for their holiday cards, the Food Shelf Program was able to generate a significant increase in annual revenues. This program was marketed in the organization's quarterly newsletter and as an insert in its direct mail program. Although this program had a modest beginning, today hundreds of boxes of cards are sold and thousands of dollars in revenues are generated.

Women's Organization Mother's Day Program

What better way to honor the special women in your life than through a Mother's Day tribute program? This promotion fit well for a women's organization from Minneapolis-St. Paul. They developed a brochure that provided different ways to honor an individual's grandmother, mother, or other favorite female. Each level of giving provided a premium that would be sent to the honored individual. This included a card at the $25 level and more elaborate gifts at higher levels. Other organizations also use the tribute idea to build higher levels of giving, offering premiums such as a book or memento, for higher gift levels.

Some organizations have used premiums donated by businesses in the community. This works well in some situations, as long as there are a sufficient number of premium gifts available to meet the demand. (See Chapter 7 for other items to consider when using premiums.)

Consider other holidays, or special days. Do any fit with your organization's mission? Or, perhaps you may wish to consider creating your own special day. For more ideas, consult your local library which may have a copy of Chase's *Book of Events*. This interesting reference book contains listing of thousands of special days that are held throughout the country.

Newspaper Insert Program

A human service organization from a small community in Michigan's Upper Peninsula has effectively used newspaper inserts in publications in cities in lower Michigan to attract donor prospects to their cause. The newspaper insert has received higher readership than have direct mail campaigns in the same communities. Also, the insert allows them greater space than a direct mail package to describe their programs with photos and text and a return device and envelope.

Fund Raising is as Simple as a Pop Tab

Successful development and marketing ideas can be extremely simple and very cost efficient. A volunteer at the Ronald McDonald House of the Twin Cities came up with the idea to collect the aluminum pull tabs off the tops of beverage cans and sell them for scrap aluminum to benefit the organization. First-year efforts raised $1,000. Word of mouth expanded the program, and $10,000 was generated in the second year. Schools began to adopt the program as a math concept to show students what a "million something" is or as part of their environmental education efforts. In the third year, $20,000 was raised, as area McDonald's restaurants offered their locations as pop tab drop-off points. A marketing campaign was developed around the theme "Pull for the kids at the Ronald McDonald House."

The program now raises $80,000 a year from tens of thousands of individuals across the country and throughout the world who are making a positive action and giving to the Ronald McDonald House. By offering donors the opportunity to share the fund raising experience with others, the Ronald McDonald House is generating high visibility, greater name recognition, and a personal investment by the thousands of donors who contribute their pop tabs.

More than 300 tons of aluminum have been collected since the first pop tab was donated in 1987. By accepting donors' gifts at this minimal giving level, the Ronald McDonald House has developed a very successful fund raising project.

Review Checklist

√ Are your organization's communications easy to read and understand?

√ Are your donors given multiple opportunities for giving?

√ Are there systems in place within your organization to measure results of communication promotions, such as direct mail and telemarketing?

√ Does your organization's development manager prepare communications that are appropriate for each target audience?

√ Do your marketing communications include the entire continuum; from prospecting, welcome of new donors or members, to ongoing acknowledgment, cultivation, and upgrade of existing donors or members?

√ Do you have an ongoing program of experimentation to determine possible new, more cost-effective methods?

√ Does the organization regularly use systems to manage the addresses, information, and gift histories of individuals in its data base?

Conclusion

Every organization has unique strengths and resources. Consider your organization. Do you have a large group of volunteers with specific skills? Or, do they have time available? What are their interests? Many clever ideas develop after convening a meeting with a key volunteer group. Remember that some of the zaniest ideas have now become the hallmark of successful marketing communications!

To be successful in a one-person development shop, a variety of solicitation vehicles must be used to attract the attention and interest of donors and members. Once you attract these stakeholders to your organization's mission, you must provide them with many opportunities for renewed and upgraded gifts and closer affiliation. Make it easy for them to give and you will make it easier to raise more money, year after year.

Cost Savings

CHAPTER

8

- ■ *Bartering Goods and Services*
- ■ *The Wish List*
- ■ *Sources for In-kind Products and Services*

Introduction

Minimizing budgetary expense is just as important as raising additional dollars. Securing in-kind contributions of goods and services will help you to accomplish this. Seemingly unlimited resources of all quantities and varieties are available to organizations that clearly identify their needs and identify the best prospects for in-kind gift support.

Fund Saving Is Just as Important as Fund Raising

Many expense items in your organization's budget can be underwritten through non-cash contributions. Typical in-kind contributions often received are:

- ■ Printing services
- ■ Legal services
- ■ Accounting services
- ■ Office supplies
- ■ Office furnishings
- ■ Food items
- ■ Clothing
- ■ Toys
- ■ Books

Sources for In-kind Contributions

Hotels and motels replace furnishings in a number of rooms each year and often are good sources of bedroom furniture and bedding for residential housing programs or homeless shelters.

Food stores may donate needed fruits, vegetables, and canned goods nearing expiration dates to food shelves and dining programs. Because bakery items have a limited shelf-life, they are often donated to nonprofit causes.

Clothing manufacturers may donate last year's styles for a kid's or adult's fashion show. One nonprofit organization has capitalized on their contacts to create a successful, full-day shopping event to secure additional revenues.

Cultivate relationships with sales representatives of quality merchandise. One sales representative often knows many other contacts within or outside of their own field. These individuals are fabulous connections for auctions and special event sales. Sales representatives also make good organizers for this type of event because they are able to solicit the support of others.

Manufacturers and major retailers may have sample seed packages, perfumes, and various food items you can use as prizes for charity events and auctions or as volunteer gifts.

Department stores may make available slightly damaged furnishings and appliances for use by community nonprofit agencies. Some major chain stores have large amounts of goods that were stolen by shoplifters, used as evidence in trials, and then made available to community organizations for their programs.

Book and magazine publishers have dated or discontinued publications that may be available to educational institutions or community literacy programs.

Sources for In-kind Services

In an era of corporate rightsizing and tight financial budgets it is more

---

Case Example

Consider the story of the Ronald McDonald House of Minneapolis-St. Paul. Their annual savings from donated services and supplies amounts to thousands of dollars. They receive an annual supply of paper products from Scott Paper Company; Coca Cola and 7-Up deliver free beverages for vending machines; Sears Carpet Cleaning cleans carpets in the three housing units twice each year; McGarvey Coffee Company donates all of the coffee for the residents of the House; and Dupont Carpeting has completely re-carpeted the entire housing complex. Even the trash hauler donates free trash pick-up at a bottom line savings of $3,000 a year.

important than ever for nonprofit organizations to offer creative ways in which corporate funders can continue to support needed community services and programs.

Although a company may have restricted dollars for charitable contributions, it may have an in-house print shop that can schedule print jobs for nonprofit brochures, annual appeals, event invitations, and annual reports.

A corporation that has undergone severe rightsizing of its work staff may be an ideal prospect for nonprofit organizations to solicit contributions of no-longer-needed office furniture, copiers, computers, audio visual equipment, and office supplies.

Even if a corporate funder can no longer sustain its financial commitment to a nonprofit organization, it may be able to donate the creative talents of its public relations or advertising departments, the accounting capabilities of its finance department, the use of its auditorium for an annual meeting, access to its phone bank for a telemarketing campaign, or office space for community programs and meetings.

Barter and Joint Purchasing Agreements

Other nonprofit organizations may also be a source of needed resources.

By developing a communications network with other local nonprofit organizations, your organization may barter an overabundance of one donated item for another item received by a different organization. For example, your organization may receive 100 cases of copy paper and may be able to trade 25 cases to another organization for a file cabinet. Your local churches, United Ways, or nonprofit group associations may be willing to publish an "Exchange Column" in their newsletter or newspaper as a community service.

Charitable organizations in the community may be willing to donate or trade the use of their kitchen and dining hall for a volunteer recognition event, their conference room for a board meeting, or their audio visual equipment for a special presentation to donor prospects. By using these resources within the community, your organization may reduce substantially the costs of its programs and events.

Equipment and supplies are also available to nonprofit organizations through national organizations such as NAEIR (The National Association for the Exchange of Industrial Resources.) NAEIR is a national clearinghouse for vast amounts of donated goods. NAEIR sends catalogs to member organizations listing the latest donated items that it has available. Items are given without charge, on a first-come, first-served basis. The nonprofit organization is charged only the shipping costs from the warehouse in Galesburg, Illinois. In order to qualify for free goods, however, the organization is charged $645 for a yearly membership. Some organizations find this sum of money a small fee for the large quantities of goods received and the overall cost savings. For information contact:

NAEIR
560 McClure St., P.O. Box 8076
Galesburg IL, 61402-8076.
[800] 562-0955

Buying in bulk or as a group often helps organizations to obtain substantial discounts. If you are part of a larger network of nonprofit groups you might consider negotiating a group purchase agreement. These are used for many types of purchases, from insurance and benefit packages, to paper and equipment.

The Wish List

Resources are available to nonprofit organizations that identify their needs and make these needs known to prospective donors. One of the best tools to use for the donation of in-kind resources is the publication and distribution of a wish list. A wish list identifies the many needs of an organization, from paper clips and typing paper to computers, vans, office buildings, and professional services.

Involve all of the organization's staff and key volunteers in the preparation of the wish list. This process allows everyone the opportunity to identify their own needs within the organization and to share their dreams of what goods and services they would ideally like to receive. The wish list should be published and updated regularly, identifying immediate needs as well as longer-term dreams. This allows the contributor to focus on the organization's most pressing needs while at the same time becoming aware of the greater needs of the organization. Sometimes if donors have appropriate community contacts, they will "go to work" for the organization in securing some of these long term needs.

Disseminate the wish list among staff, volunteers, service recipients, contributors, and donor prospects. Distribute it by newsletter or flyer, or include it in your organization's annual report. A wish list is also a valuable tool for donor solicitation calls. It can be shared with donors or prospects who may not be able to make a current cash contribution but would like to know about other ways in which they could help your organization.

Unless your organization is willing to accept any contribution of in-kind goods and services, it is especially important to be very specific about the type, make, model, size, shape, color, and styles that you need. This will help your organization avoid a potentially embarrassing situation of refusing a donor's gift or having to immediately dispose of the donated items after their receipt.

For example, if a local hospital is soliciting dolls to give to young patients during the holidays, it should be very explicit that they need to be new and in their original packaging. Otherwise, the hospital can almost be guaranteed of receiving a vast assortment of very used dolls found in basements and attics.

Another point to consider is that some contributors will use nonprofit organizations as dumping grounds for goods and materials that have little use, other than as a tax deduction for the donor. Your very explicit wish list will assist your organization in saying no to donations that are not appropriate.

Sample Wish List

Immediate Needs

Office Supplies
white copy paper
4 staplers
4 boxes of staples
1 three-hole punch
colored construction paper

Office Equipment
3 swivel desk chairs
2 computer stands
5 waste baskets
4 desk lamps
6 three-drawer file cabinets

Dream List Needs

Equipment
1 nine-passenger van
2 IBM Pentium 100 computers
2 HP Laser Printers
office space

Services
annual financial audit
printing of annual report
production of promotional video
marketing focus groups

Conclusion

The old axiom of "a penny saved is a penny earned" is essential for a nonprofit organization with limited resources. Many donors who are unable to contribute cash to your organization can become instrumental donors by donating equipment, supplies, and professional skills.

Reducing costs will also help your organization preserve its assets to carry out your important programs and services.

A wish list also encourages community organizations and service clubs to become involved in your organization. Local Jaycees, Rotary Clubs, and churches or synagogues may use the wish list to fulfill a service requirement. A wish list is also an ideal opportunity to involve young people. Although youth often do not have the financial means to support a local charity, they do have energy, enthusiasm, and a willingness to serve. Youth groups such as Boy Scouts, Girl Scouts, and 4-H may use the wish list as a challenge for a service requirement or as a fun social event as they go on a scavenger hunt to help a charitable cause.

The wish list is also a public relations tool, as it increases name recognition and public awareness for your organization.

Review Checklist

√   Have you explored opportunities for in-kind gifts?

√   Are there any opportunities with other nonprofit organizations, schools, or businesses for joint purchases, or barter of services and/or products?

√   Does your organization communicate its needs to its publics in a way that encourages giving and referral to appropriate resources?

Acknowledgment & Recognition

CHAPTER

9

■ *Donor and Volunteer Acknowledgment*

■ *Donor and Volunteer Recognition*

Introduction

Saying thank-you to donors, members, and volunteers and recognizing their special contributions is among the top priorities for the development manager. Although this seems like a simple task, many nonprofit organizations do not feel that they have the resources of time, money, or staff to recognize all supporters of their organization. This chapter will identify ways in which even the one-person development shop can successfully carry out these important development functions.

Donor and Volunteer Acknowledgment

Timely and appropriate acknowledgment of donors' gifts is an essential ingredient in cultivating the long-term interest and commitment of donors. It is important to thank donors again and again. Whether it be a personalized letter, handwritten note, pre-printed card, computerized receipt, telephone call, or personal meeting, it is fundamental that you continue to thank your donors.

It is surprising how many organizations do not take the time or make the expenditure required to show appreciation to those who support them. Many organizations set minimum gift levels that donors must achieve before the development office feels it can justify the expense of acknowledgment. They may be correct in telling donors that their canceled check is their receipt but a canceled check is no indication of gratitude on the part of the nonprofit organization. Should all gifts to your organization be acknowledged? Yes! Should all donors be acknowledged in the same manner? No!

Gift Clubs

Just as you segment individuals for solicitation, you may also segment them for purposes of acknowledgment and recognition. By establishing gift clubs that provide appropriate forms of acknowledgment and recognition for different levels of giving, you can also create incentives for donors to upgrade their gifts.

You may be familiar with the use of gift clubs by organizations such as public radio and public television which offer various incentives for different levels of giving. Similarly, you can use different forms of acknowledgment and recognition for donors and volunteers who achieve different levels of contributions annually and/or cumulatively over a lifetime.

See the following illustration for a sample gift club acknowledgment and recognition program.

The development office maintains responsibility for timely and appropriate donor acknowledgment. Still, many people within the organization, including staff, board members, volunteers, and key donors, must play an integral role in conducting the ongoing acknowledgment process.

Illustration 21: Gift Club Acknowledgment

Gift Club	Donor Level	Acknowledgment/Recognition Procedure
Friend	$1.00-$24.99	Pre-printed acknowledgment card signed by volunteer. Listed in newsletter.
Sponsor	$25.00 - $99.99	Form letter signed by executive director. Listed in newsletter and annual report.
Benefactor	$100.00 - $249.99	Hand-written note by executive director. Listed in newsletter and annual report. Appreciation certificate.
Executive Circle	$250.00 - $999.99	Call from executive director or member of board. Personalized thank-you letter signed by board president. Listed in newsletter and annual report. Appreciation certificate prepared by calligrapher.
President's Roundtable	$1,000.00 and above	Call from executive director. Personal thank you letter from board president. Acknowledgment letter signed by executive director. Listed in newsletter. Featured in annual report. Recognition plaque.

Timeliness of Acknowledgment

Ideally a donor should be acknowledged within 24-48 hours after their gift is received. While this turnaround time may seem almost impossible to a small development program with limited staff and resources, it quickly can become a standard procedure with a little planning, creativity, and resourcefulness.

The most important factor to remember when managing a donor acknowledgment process is to thank the donor. Period!

As a development professional, you may want to send every donor a personalized acknowledgment signed by your executive director or board chair. Yet, you must be realistic about your capabilities and recognize your limitations. The most important factor to remember when managing a donor acknowledgment process is to thank the donor. Period!

Who thanks the donor and how the donor is thanked is secondary to the basic need to thank him or her soon after the gift is received. Again, you cannot do it all alone. You must recruit the assistance of volunteers, staff, board members, donors, and even your program recipients to share in this effort.

Time-Saving Acknowledgment Cards

Pre-printed postcards or cards that can be inserted into envelopes facilitate the acknowledgment process for the majority of gifts. This is especially useful for smaller gifts. The cards can carry a brief message referring to the important mission of the organization and how the donor's gift will be used. A photo of a program recipient or a testimonial quote referring to the organization may also be included.

The card should allow space for personalization of the salutation that can be written or typed on the card. The amount of the donor's gift should also be stated on the card. Some organizations pre-print a variety of cards or letters stating various amounts while others print only one style of card, leaving the gift amount space blank to be filled in by the staff or volunteer. The card should also be signed by the person acknowledging the gift. Ideally, the card should allow space for a brief handwritten note. (For example, "As a volunteer with People Helping People I want you to know how much I appreciate your support for this important program.") You can practice the concept of *high tech, high touch* by incorporating this small human touch to what otherwise could be perceived as a cost effective but somewhat cold acknowledgment response.

Form Letters

Letters are a more personal approach to donors and give your organization the image of a very professional operation. A variety of letter templates can be prepared in advance to recognize various levels of giving. Volunteers, staff, interns, or even the people you serve can write the text for the letters of thanks. Computer technologies now allow you greater opportunities than ever to personalize form thank-you letters to your donors. By using mail-merge procedures you can prepare batches of personalized acknowledgments to your donors immediately after their gifts are received.

However, when using form letter acknowledgments, you should have a system to identify donors who make repeated gifts so that they do not continue to receive the same letter. Similarly, you should provide variation in your acknowledgments to monthly donors or you will damage your professional image and the goodwill intended in your acknowledgment process. Setting up a tracking system for form-type acknowledgment is advisable.

Personal Letters and Notes

Perhaps the most appreciated form of written acknowledgment is a personal letter or handwritten note recognizing the donor's unique and special contributions to the organization. Unfortunately, this is also the most labor-intensive form of written communication. While you may not be able to provide this type of acknowledgment to all donors for each gift, you do

need to take the time to use this type of communication with special, major, and long-term donors.

You can save time by delegating donor names to the executive director, program staff, board members, volunteers, key donors, and program participants. A little creativity and variety on the part of the development staff may be especially appreciated by the acknowledged donor. For instance, a donor who has long been acknowledged by the executive director each time a gift has been given may instead receive a personal note from a person who has directly benefited from the programs and services of your organization. A personal note from a program recipient will usually generate tremendous good will with a donor and will also elevate their commitment to the organization.

Telephone Calls

Does this scenario sound familiar? You are in the final week of planning a major special event, the budget is due in two weeks, you are trying to finalize the year-end campaign, and your other duties are consuming every available minute. In the middle of this chaos, an envelope arrives with a check for $500 from a donor/member who has previously only given gifts of $50. You are elated and want to write a personal note to the donor in appreciation. However, your other duties demand your time and you know you won't be able to write an appropriate response for a couple of weeks. Don't delay your acknowledgment! Pick up the telephone, call the donor, tell the donor that you just received the check and you couldn't wait to express your thanks for the tremendous gift and for the donor's continued support. Let the donor hear your words of excitement and appreciation. In two or three minutes time you will have shared more with your donor than any letter ever has and you will have acknowledged the gift in a timely and appropriate manner. This allows you to continue with your other tasks without the feelings of guilt for not acknowledging this special contribution.

Telephone acknowledgments are quick, effective, and extremely personal ways to show your donors that you received their gifts, you appreciate their support, and you encourage their continued involvement with your organization. These verbal acknowledgments should always be followed with a written acknowledgment for the donor's records and as a reinforcement of the words of appreciation that they personally received by phone.

In addition to recognizing donors for special or unique gifts, you may also incorporate telephone acknowledgments into your overall acknowledgment program. You may wish to designate your executive director or board chair to call all donors at certain giving levels or those who have given support to special programs.

Brief telephone acknowledgment allows donors to hear firsthand how important their gifts are to your organization. The call may also uncover valuable information about the donor that will assist you in your cultivation efforts. A donor may inform you that he made a larger gift because he just received a large inheritance (potential for additional support for a special program or project), or a new donor giving you a large gift may state that she heard about your program for children and since she never married or had any children she would like to do something to help families and children (potential for planned giving program.) Similarly, a young couple might tell you that they were happy to send the check but were wondering if there were any other ways in which they could assist your organization (potential volunteers.)

Telephone thank-you programs can also be established to reach special donors. Many organizations enlist volunteers to conduct an annual telephone thank-you campaign. Volunteers are assigned a number of donors to call to simply say "thank you for your support." There is no solicitation, no request for increased involvement, just a simple thank you. Donors may be surprised by such a call because they suspect there is another motive. However, when they realize that they are being called only to be thanked, they are very pleased by the gesture and are more likely to think favorably of your organization the next time they receive a request for support.

Personal Meetings

Personal meetings with key donors or members are effective in providing acknowledgment. These meetings normally will follow the timely letter or phone call immediately after receipt of their gift. Naturally, personal meetings are not feasible for very many of your donors. Nonetheless, for those special donors who you really want to cultivate and involve more in your organization, a personal meeting in their office, home, or at a restaurant or club can pay lasting dividends. By delegating these personal calls to your executive director, members of the board, key volunteers, and major donors you can reach a larger number of donors and develop relationships with them. If time allows, you may wish to join these representatives as they meet with donors. Or, you may wish to invite some of your volunteers or program recipients to join you in these personal meetings, to share their experiences and appreciation with the donors.

Personally meeting with donors will assist you in learning more about their commitment to your organization, as well as give you background on their family, their work, their personal interests, and the other organizations and causes which they support. A one-to-one conversation with key donors will also help you to discover more about how they became involved with your organization, what has motivated them to give, what concerns they might have about your programs or operations, and how passionate they are about your mission.

Making observations of their office or home can also tell you much more about the donor. For instance do they have family pictures on the desk or walls? (This may indicate that family and children are important to them and may be a special focus for their giving.) Do they have sports trophies or awards? (This may provide good ideas for future cultivation or recognition efforts.) For example, inviting an avid golfer to join you in a round of golf or recognizing a donor by presenting a special fishing lure to an avid angler can be effective ways to nurture the relationship between the donor and your organization.)Have the donors received recognition plaques or certificates from other nonprofit organizations? (This may assist you in determining their other charitable interests and also how they like to be recognized.)

You may be asking "How can I find the time for personal meetings?"

When donors realize that they are being called only to be thanked, they are very pleased by the gesture and are more likely to think favorably of your organization the next time they receive a request for support.

Many development staff often plan ahead and have their lunch hour with a special donor or member. Yes, you should be taking time for lunch, just as others should!

Volunteer Acknowledgment

Sometimes you may get so busy acknowledging your financial contributors that you forget to acknowledge the contributions of those people who are most involved in your day-to-day program and development activities—your volunteers.

Volunteers working in your office or on special fund raising projects should be thanked every time you see them. Arrange a luncheon to celebrate an individual's years of service. Or, just say a simple "thank you for your work today" or "thanks for soliciting those silent auction items last week." These are words that volunteers greatly appreciate. You will motivate them to continue to serve you and your organization.

A simple post-it note stating "We really appreciate all that you are doing for us" attached to a volunteer's work assignments can really be an uplifting way to help him or her start their day.

Donor/Member/Volunteer Recognition

Recognition of your donors and volunteers allows you to thank them again and again for their special contributions to your organization. Recognition may take many forms. Some may be special one-time events

---

Case Example

Little Brothers - Friends of the Elderly in Minneapolis has adopted a very inexpensive but most effective manner in which to thank their key donors personally. One day each year they enlist the involvement of board members and volunteers to deliver a long-stemmed rose to each of their key contributors with a personal message of thanks for their support. In addition to the appreciation the donors feel by this unique acknowledgment, the gift of roses has also increased visibility for the organization in the donor's workplace as coworkers inquire why the individual received a lovely rose. The organization has been able to get the roses donated by a local florist and all deliveries supplied by the organization's volunteers.

while others may be lasting forms of recognition that pay tribute to your contributors in perpetuity. Recognition also allows you the opportunity to publicly acknowledge the special contributions of money, time, and talent that your volunteers and donors provide.

Newsletters

One of the most common forms of donor recognition is a listing of donor and volunteer names in newsletters. This is an easy and effective way to pay tribute to those who have contributed to the organization during the past month, quarter, or year. Donors and volunteers can be segmented by gift levels or project involvement. Some individuals may appear in both lists. While this may seem redundant it is important to recognize individuals for all of their contributions. And who has ever complained about being thanked too often?

Some organizations may not feel they have the financial resources to pay for extra recognition pages in their newsletters. But successful development offices often find their investment to be repaid over and over by the goodwill and continued support that public recognition provides.

Photos of volunteers or key donors in the newsletter are also especially effective forms of recognition and promotional tools. A photograph of volunteers working at the finish line of your 5K benefit run or of an individual putting the final touches on table decorations for the annual dinner dance can inspire others to become involved. A photo of a corporate president presenting an enlarged check to your organization or a shot of a civic club delivering a truckload of items that were listed on your wish list can motivate others to consider similar gifts. Photo recognition can also pay tribute to committee members heading up your capital campaign or welcoming new members of the development committee. Remember to provide extra copies of newsletters to people pictured in the photos. They will be very proud of this recognition and very happy to share the newsletter with their friends and associates, who in turn may also become involved with your organization.

Annual Report

An annual report is an excellent vehicle for reaching your internal and external audiences and effectively recognizing those who support your organization. Design the report so that it is easy to read for all of your key publics. Use plenty of photos, graphics and captions to communicate key messages. In this manner, even if an individual cannot take the time to read the entire report, he or she will still pick up important information.

Newsletters are an easy and effective way to pay tribute to those who have contributed to the organization during the past month, quarter, or year.

Some organizations that do not list donors in newsletters use the annual report for this form of recognition. Other organizations compile the lists from their newsletters and print them again in their annual report. Again, it is a question of financial resources when it comes to the cost of listing all donors and volunteers in the annual report. While some organizations only list major donors in this annual publication, small development shops will likely find greater success if they can print the names of *all* donors and volunteers.

The annual report also provides an excellent communications vehicle for recognizing key supporters through photographs and feature articles about their contributions. A feature story on a long-term donor who made a lead gift on the endowment program not only recognizes this gift publicly but also encourages other donors or donor prospects to consider a similar gift.

Low-Cost Variations for Plaques and Certificates

Plaques and certificates are an effective means to present key donors and volunteers with a form of recognition that will last for many years.

Although these recognition pieces are very special and meaningful to the recipient, they can be costly and even

---

Case Examples

A social service agency serving the elderly has used photographs of smiling elderly program participants pasted on a personalized certificate prepared on a word processor. The photo and certificate is then placed in an inexpensive frame for a one-of-a-kind donor recognition award.

A health care agency has printed appreciation certificates for donors and volunteers that leave blank spaces for names and the contributions that are being recognized. The development office types the name and contribution on a computer and then runs the certificates through the printer for a quick, easy, personalized, and very professional-looking recognition certificate.

prohibitive for many small development programs.

Some small development shops have overcome these economic obstacles by developing creative variations on this form of recognition.

You may wish to enlist the contributions of volunteer calligraphers or artists to prepare special recognition certificates for your important donors. Or you may even enlist the talents of children to say thank you through their artwork or the kind words of an adult program recipient written on a brief letter or note that is put into a decorative frame.

Donor Walls

A more permanent form of donor recognition is often seen in lobbies of nonprofit organizations. The donor wall is usually a more formalized vehicle for recognizing the special contributions of donors and volunteers. Some organizations have incorporated the tree of life model where donors are given an engraved leaf on a tree of contributors. A social service agency in Phoenix has developed a local version of this concept by creating a cactus with arms listing the individual donors.

Case Example

The Mayo Clinic in Rochester, Minnesota, has incorporated interactive television with their donor hall of tribute. In addition to plaques and certificates recognizing the contributions of major donors, they also have videotaped testimonials from endowment donors stating why they have supported Mayo Clinic through their planned gift. Visitors can view these testimonials simply by touching the screen and bringing up the video of the particular donor . In addition, all donors are listed by city, state, and country, so visitors to the donor room can find out who else from their hometown or country is a contributor to the clinic.

Although many organizations recognize one-time major gifts to capital or endowment campaigns on their donor walls, other organizations have found it effective to recognize donors' cumulative giving on donor plaques that can be updated from year to year. Using gift clubs can greatly assist your development office.

An affordable means to secure special mementos for your donors and volunteers is to use the creative talents of your volunteers and program recipients.

Other organizations have developed large wall plaques or stand-alone murals that list donors and volunteers on brass plates, engraved wood, or typeset poster boards. Whatever the vehicle, it is important for your nonprofit organization to adopt some form of permanent recognition for your key supporters. It not only strengthens your relationship with your donors and volunteers but also serves as an important public relations tool for educating and inspiring to others who visit your office.

Special Mementos

As you develop your relationship with key donors and volunteers and learn more about their personal likes and interests you can develop more

specialized forms of recognition. Some organizations have commissioned paintings and drawings, produced crystal bowls and platters, and designed unique trophies, medals, coins, and awards. These can be very special and memorable mementos for your donors to receive in appreciation for their lasting contributions to your organization. However, for many small development programs, the costs for these recognition items are not feasible.

An affordable means to secure special mementos for your donors and volunteers is to use the creative talents of your volunteers and program recipients. Recruit those who sew, knit, or do crafts. Then, have this creative individual present the gift to the special volunteer, on behalf of your

Case Example

A small youth service agency was able to enlist their volunteers in planning and conducting their own recognition event. The thirty volunteers who assisted in the office during the year organized a potluck luncheon. Volunteers each brought a food item to share at the celebration. The assembly room was decorated with balloons, the tables had flowers and candles, and the volunteers had a great time in this celebration of their joint efforts. Several key volunteers were recognized before the group and all volunteers received an appreciation certificate.

organization. They will assist you in your development efforts by helping you to provide a unique and special acknowledgment award.

Recognition Events

Annual recognition events provide an opportunity to publicly thank key donors and volunteers and celebrate with them the achievements and success of your organization. Recognition events can take many forms, from annual galas to very informal luncheons, picnics, or days at the ball park.

Small development offices operating with a limited budget can be very creative in structuring their annual recognition events. Recognition events should be fun celebrations. They should also fit with the culture of your organization. An expensive recognition event will not be appreciated by donors and volunteers who know that the organization is operating on a tight budget and who believe that funding should go to support programs and services rather than to elaborate recognition of their contributions.

Planning and conducting appropriate recognition events does not have to be the sole responsibility of the development staff. Include your volunteers and donors. They too enjoy thanking others for their contributions and will be of great assistance

to you in carrying out this important development function.

Review Checklist

√ Is acknowledgment timely (within 24-48 hours)?

√ Are there regular programs in place to acknowledge volunteers?

√ Has your organization explored alternatives to written acknowledgments to encourage public and/or more personalized acknowledgments?

√ Have you recruited board, volunteers, and staff to help you?

Conclusion

Acknowledgment and recognition is not a one-time event but rather an ongoing process of thanking your donors and volunteers. By determining the frequency and appropriateness of the form of acknowledgment and recognition for your contributors you can express your appreciation for their involvement and support and continue to cultivate their interest in your organization.

ORDER FORM

If you enjoyed *Fund Raising & Marketing in the One-Person Shop*, perhaps you'd like to order another copy for a colleague, board member, volunteer, or friend.

Please check all that apply:

_____ Please send (quantity) copies of *Fund Raising & Marketing in the One-person Shop*.

Method of payment;
        ___*Check or money order enclosed for: $ 29.95*
                                  $ 4.00 shipping/handling
        Minnesota residents add sales tax $ 2.10
        *or provide tax exempt number   **Total** **$ 36.05***

        VISA, MASTERCARD or credit card orders call BookMasters at: 1-800-247-6553.

_____*Please contact me about a discount on quantity sales.*

_____*Please contact me about Henley & Hodiak's training and/or consulting services.*

      Your name   _____
      Street   _____
      City, state, zip   _____
      Phone number _____
      Fax number   _____

_____*Please add my friend or colleague's name to your mailing list so that you can notify*
      them of your book:

      Your name   _____
      Street   _____
      City, state, zip   _____
      Phone number _____
      Fax number   _____

Send to:

      Development Resource Center
      4744 10th Avenue South
      Mpls, MN 55407-3504   612-929-6737   fax 612-824-5762

INDEX

A

Acknowledgment 147, 178, 179, 180, 181, 182, 184
Acknowledgment cards 180
ACORN 160
Acquisition 146, 147
ADDRESS CORRECTION REQUESTED 159
Advertising 109
America Online 34
Annual report 15, 18, 166, 175, 185, 186
Annuities 125
Appended 156
Appending information to database 160
Assignment editor 96
Auctions 173
Automation Compatible Mail 156

B

Back end premiums 162
Backgrounders 91
Barcodes 145,5-156
Barter 174
BAUD rates, 34
Bequest 125, 127
Billboard 105, 106
BIOGRAPH 24
Board member 87
Board member job description 86
Board orientation 85
Bookmarks 111
Bulletins 107

C

CACI Marketing Systems 160
Card deck advertising 167
CASE (see Council for the Advancement and Support of Education)
Case for support 29, 48
CASS CERTIFICATION 155-156
Catalog of Federal Domestic Assistance 22–23
Cause related marketing 114
CD-Rom 40
CDI (Compact Disc Interactive) 41
Census data, 50
Certificates 186
Charitable lead trust 126
Charitable remainder trust 126
Chief executive 3
Children's Cancer Research Fund 10
Child's Play Theater Company 62, 69
Collaboration, 10–12

Communication insert 167
Communication plan 122
Communication strategy 62, 69
Community foundations 127
Comparative results 57
Competitor analysis 46, 46–47, 52
Competitors (perceived) 52
Compiled lists 150
CompuMentor 30
CompuServe 24, 34, 35
Computer hardware 31
Computer publication 29
Computer server 36
Computer technical support 29
Computer technologies 181
Constituency Circle 53
Continuation 152
Contribution envelope 166
Contribution forms 166
"Core" donors 120
Corporate sponsors 11
Council for Advancement and Support of Education (CASE) 167
Credit card 88, 166
Credit card pledge 166
Crisis management 88, 90
Cross promotions 113
Cultivation 3, 20, 183
Current donors 74, 84
Customized software systems 31

D

Deceased file 156
Deliverability 151
DEMOGRAPHICS (file at Knight Ridder Information Systems) 24
Digital cameras 40
Direct mail solicitations 166
Direct Marketing Association 153
Discretionary funds 12
Display advertising 105
Donated software 29
Donnelly, Inc 160
Donor giving clubs 123
Donor hall of tribute 187
Donor profile 14
Donor recognition events 4
Donor segment 84
Donor segmentation strategies 82
Dun & Bradstreet Market Identifiers 24
Dun & Bradstreet Million Dollar Directory, 24

E

E-mail 33
East-West EducationDevelopment

Foundation 30
Electronic fund transfer 88, 142
Employee giving 87, 88
Endowment 186, 187
Environmental audit 127
ERIC database 22
Evaluation systems 57
Event calendars 101

F

Fairs 111
Feature article 101, 102, 186
Federal Access Programs Retrieval System 22–24
Federal Register Abstracts (FRA) 23–24
Focus groups 15, 163
Form 990's (see IRS Form 990's)
Form letters 180, 181
Foundation Directory (The) 23
Foundation Grants Index (FGI) 23
Fraternal organizations 12
Free advertising space 101
Front end premiums 162
Fulfillment 143, 147
Fund raising software 27, 31

G

Gift annuities 126
Gift "asks," 20
Gift clubs 163, 178, 179
Gifts in Kind America 30
Giving pyramid 119
Global Recycling Network 30

H

Home pages 36, 39
HTML 39
Hyatt Regency's "World's Largest Office Party," 12

I

IRS form 990's 18, 48
In-kind
    contributions 172
    goods and services 173, 176
    resources 175
    services 173
Incentives 16
Individual gifts 119
INFOTRAC, 17
In-house print shops 174
Institute for Global Communications 35
Interactive television 40, 187
Internet 32, 33, 36

Internships 9–12
Interview 100
IQUEST 24
IRS determination letter 48

J

Jaycees 12
Job descriptions 9
Joint purchasing agreements 174

K

Key codes 144
Key Competitor Analysis 52
Key Public Matrix 70
Key publics 61, 62, 64, 69, 103
Key spokesperson 90
Key stakeholders 62
Kiwanis clubs 12
Knight-Ridder Information 23–24

L

Lapsed donors 75
Lead gift 186
Letters to the Editor 103
LEXUS 17
Life income gifts 125
Life insurance 125, 126
List broker 153, 154
Lists or information booklets 113
LYBNT donors 73, 84

M

Mail-merge 181
Mailroom Companion, (U.S. Postal
      Service) 155-156
Major donors 123, 124, 187
Major gifts 119, 162
          program 122
Market research 14
Marketing communications 61, 62, 103,
      104
Marquis Who's Who Directories 24
Marriage mail 167
Matching gifts 166, 167
Media 91
          advisory letter 94, 95
          contacts 99
          interviews 102
          personnel list 96
          service companies 99
Mementos 188
Memorial 168
Merge-purge 153
Microsoft Network 34, 35

Mini rulers 111
Mini-surveys 15
Mission 49, 69
Mission statement 46, 47, 49, 69
Modem 34, 40
Movie theaters 107
Multivariate statistics 156

N

NAEIR 174, 175
National Change of Address 155
National Cristina Foundation 30
National Data Book 24
National Football League 12
National Society of Fund Raising Execu-
      tives (NSFRE) 13
Networking 12
Newsletters 15, 83, 107, 166, 185, 186
Newspaper inserts 169
Newswires 96
NEXUS 17
Nominating committee of the board 9, 10
Nonprofit Computing 30
Nonprofit Organization's New Media Center
      40
Notes (for volunteer recognition) 181
"Notice of Proposed Rulemaking" 22

O

OCR Scanners 40
ONESEARCH 24
Optical character reading, scanners 40
Ornaments 113
ORYX Press 24
Outsourcing 156
Overlay 156

P

Payroll deduction programs 88, 143
PEOPLE 24
Personal letters 181
Personal meetings 183
Photographs 186
Piggyback programs 168
Planned giving 123, 124, 125, 126, 127
      182
Plaques 186, 188
Pledge card 136
Pledge reminder 166
Pop tab 169
Premium 162, 163, 169
Press kit 100, 102
Press mailing 99
Press release 94, 102
Print media 101
Pro-bono 92

Prodigy 24, 34, 35
Product packaging 108
Prospect rating form 21, 120
Prospecting program 19
Prospect research committee. 20
Protocol sheet 94
Psycho-graphic information 159-161
Public recognition 185
Public relations 61, 91, 177
          campaign 92–94, 96
          plan 69
Public service announcements 96
PYBNT donors 84

Q

Quick and dirty surveys 58

R

Readerboards 106
Real estate (donations) 127
Recognition
      3, 88, 178, 179, 183, 184, 185,
      186, 187
          events 189
Recruiters 6
Recyclable items 30
Refrigerator magnets 111
Reply device 166
Revenue goals (setting realistic) 45
Response list 149
Rule of three 102

S

Sectional Center Facility 161
Securities (donation) 126
Segmentation 57, 76, 83, 84, 178
Segmenting the database 57
Service clubs 77
Service configuration matrix 53
Service delivery system 52
Shopping center signs 107
Software communications program 34
Sororities 12
Source Book Profiles 23–24
Speaker's bureau. 4, 85
Special events 6, 114-117
Specialized forms of recognition 188
Sponsors 18
Stakeholders 53, 69
Standard & Poor's Register 24
Standard Rate and Data Service 151, 154
State Attorney General's office 18
Statement of Volunteer Responsibilities 7
Statement stuffers 106
Stickers and decals 111

Strategic plan 2, 44, 46, 47
Survey 58, 163
      biases 58
      data 50
      mini 15
SWOT analysis 46–47, 49, 50, 51

T

Target public 92
Technical assistance 30
Technical support 31
Telemarketing 83, 151, 163
Telemarketing campaigns 164-166
Telemarketing job position 6
Telephone acknowledgments 182
Telephone calls 181
Telephone surveys 14–15
(also, see surveys)
Testimonials 49, 187
Trade shows 111
Training 28, 110
Tribute programs 168, 169, 185
Trust 125

U

United Way 89
Unrelated business income 162
Usenet groups 33
User groups 28

V

Vendor 76
Veteran's of Foreign Wars 12
Video productions 110
Video tapes 108
Volunteer acknowledgment 184
Volunteer Bill of Rights 7
Volunteer opportunities 6
Volunteers 5

W

Web site 39
Web programming language (HTML) 39
"Welcome to the organization" package 84
Will 125
Wish list 32, 175, 176, 177
Working and standing committees (board)
    9
World Wide Web 36
Written acknowledgment 182
Written Surveys 15 (also, see surveys)